RED HERRINGS
AND
WHITE ELEPHANTS

RED HERRINGS
AND
WHITE ELEPHANTS

ALBERT JACK

WITH ILLUSTRATIONS
BY AMA PAGE

metro

Published by Metro Publishing Ltd
an imprint of John Blake Publishing,
3 Bramber Court, 2 Bramber Road,
London W14 9PB, England

www.blake.co.uk

First published in paperback in 2007

ISBN: 978 1 84454 461 5

British Library Cataloguing-in-Publication Data:

A catalogue record for this book is available from the British Library.

Design by www.envydesign.co.uk

Printed in Great Britain by Mackays of Chatham Ltd, Chatham, Kent

1 3 5 7 9 10 8 6 4 2

Papers used by Metro Publishing are natural, recyclable products
made from wood grown in sustainable forests. The manufacturing
processes conform to the environmental regulations of the
country of origin.

Every attempt has been made to contact the relevant copyright-holders,
but some were unobtainable. We would be grateful if the appropriate
people could contact us.

This book is dedicated to the memory of
Albert Victor Childs (1916–1998)

CONTENTS

ACKNOWLEDGEMENTS

Thanks in the first place go to Martyn Long whose trivial conversation at the inns around Guildford sparked the idea in the first place. That master of triviality then provided enough inspiration for me to crawl through dirty libraries with dusty librarians (although in some cases that was the other way round) and research the origin of some of our favourite phrases.

Special thanks also go to Ama Page, all the way out there in Botswana, for the wonderful illustrations and to Tony Banks MP for offering to host the book launch in the House (and I don't mean his house).

Normal thanks go to the following for contributing

ideas, answers, leads and suggestions. In no particular order, then: Andy McDaniel and Denise Hance; Bruce Foxton and Steve Grantley of the Stiff Little Fingers fame (make of that what you will) who are responsible for a couple of the little gems you will later read. Then thanks to Claire Miller for the illustration of me; the Bailey Teswaine trio of Peter Patsalides for the Greek translation, Paul Ryan for his spiritual guidance and fatherly advice and Tony Henderson for all his support; Nigel Harland for lunch at the Lords, followed by the Commons and then followed by a visit to their respective libraries. (No dusty librarians in there, then).

It should also be recorded that David Dickie's suggestions (set enough traps in the woods and you are going to catch a badger) weren't quite what I had in mind but made us all laugh just the same. Peter Gordon and Joe Hobbs should get a mention in here somewhere and so must my sister Julie Willmott and cousin John Harris. Thanks to Martin Foale for his suggestion, Lucian Randall and all at Blake Publishing.

If this book is a roaring success then all of them should share the credit in some small way. If, however, it turns out to be an unmitigated disaster, then they can have all the credit themselves and leave me out of it.

Albert Jack – Guildford

Albert Jack supports the MacKinnon Trust, a registered charity working to raise awareness in mental health issues such schizophrenia and the care needed by those who suffer and their families.

www.mackinnontrust.org

Albert Jack's website is at
www.albertjack.com
www.passionmonkey.com

INTRODUCTION

In the course of a day, we all use many examples of what is known as an idiom. Idioms are words and phrases which those of us with a native English tongue take for granted, as we have grown up to recognise their meaning. That is despite the words being used having absolutely nothing to do with the context of a conversation we are having.

For example, if I explained I am writing this preface 'off the cuff', you would immediately recognise it as an unprepared piece being written in one take (which, by the way, it is). But why do I call that 'off the cuff' when it has nothing to do with my cuffs, much less being either on or off them?

If I suggest everything in this book is absolutely

true, I can emphasis that statement by insisting every word in here is 'straight from the horse's mouth'. Again, we all know that means it has come directly from the source of information and is therefore reliable. But I haven't got a horse. I have never spoken to one and unless I can find one that wins more often, even when I hedge my bets, then I might have nothing to do with any of the beasts again.

These phrases appear in conversation all over the English-speaking world every minute of the day and we take them for granted. Have you ever heard someone say they had a bone to pick with you or they could smell a rat? Have you wondered what on earth they were talking about? No, probably not, because we all grow up knowing what these phrases refer to, but, if you were overheard by anyone learning our beautiful language, they'd think we were all mad.

However, have you ever wondered where those phrases come from in the first place and why we use them? I did, when I was sitting in a pub with a friend, who was feeling a little groggy and under the weather, as he had been out painting the town red the previous night. I suggested a hair of the dog was in order and the bar-person, who was an English student from Colombia, and a very good one at that, thought we were crazy. She told us dogs weren't allowed in the pub. How we all laughed.

It was wintertime, and cold enough to freeze the balls off a brass monkey, so cold, in fact, I believe it was snowing in the ladies. So we sat by the fire, hair of the dog in hand, and started wondering where those sayings originated and why they are so natural to use. The pub's guv'nor eventually fetched us up a square meal, but we'd been there a while and before we all reached the end of our tethers I decided to leave for home. It was raining cats and dogs outside, so I bit the bullet and made my way through the cold and started researching these little phrases. Within minutes I had discovered that many of them do have traceable origins and some even emerge from a particular event in history. Some are unbelievable but, by and large, many make immediate sense. Some have more than one suggested origin, in which case, I have chosen the source that had the best supporting evidence. Therefore, I can assure the reader, there is only one cock and bull story among them.

It took months of painstaking research, working

mainly between the hours of closing time and opening time, before I finally had it in the bag and the fruit of that labour is now in your hand. I know there are many missing idioms (thousands of the rascals, in fact), but we deliberately selected only the best-known sayings with interesting origins. The idea was not to create a definitive dictionary of well-known phrases, but to choose the ones we could have some fun with and those that you, the reader who sent a shilling in my direction, would enjoy.

Thanks to my brilliant illustrator, Ama Page, there are also some top-notch cartoons to help you along the way. If this volume proves to be popular, there will be a second edition to which you are invited to contribute by sending suggestions to info@albertjack.com.

But there is another benefit to reading this book. Everybody loves trivia, but nobody likes a smart Alec. So, the next time you are caught in a corner with somebody talking a load of old codswallop, tell them where that phrase comes from and then start reciting a few of the other shaggy dog tales from this collection. That should get rid of them for you.

1: NAUTICAL

To be **Taken Aback** suggests someone has been taken truly by surprise and stopped in their tracks. 'Aback' is the nautical term for sudden wind change, in which the sails flatten against the mast. In some cases, out on the high seas, tall square-rigged ships may not only be slowed down by a sudden wind change, but also driven backwards by strong gusts. The phrase used in such circumstances is 'taken aback'.

To **Batten Down The Hatches** is to prepare for trouble that is unavoidable and coming your way. Most ships and boats have cargo holds that are accessible via hatches on the decks and these are protected by lids. In times of heavy seas or approaching storms a ship's captain would call out the order to batten down these hatch lids to prevent the holds becoming full of sea or rain water. Sailors would secure the lids with lengths of batten, preventing them from flying off during a gale. The expression is known to have been in use since at least 1823.

To **Have Someone Over A Barrel** means that somebody is totally at the mercy of third parties and unable to have any influence over the circumstances surrounding them. In medieval Britain it was standard practice to drape a drowning, or drowned, person face down over a large barrel to try and clear their lungs. As the victim was usually unconscious it was obvious they were totally reliant upon third parties and whatever action they took would determine their fate. Not really an ideal situation to be in for many reasons – especially in the Navy.

The **Bitter End** is the absolute end. This phrase has its origins at sea and is nothing to do with taste. On the sailing ships of past centuries, the anchor was fixed to the deck by solid bollards

2

made of iron and wood known as 'bitts'. Coloured rags were tied to the rope near the deck end and once they were revealed crewmates knew the anchor could not be let out much further. The rope between the anchor and rag was known as the bitt end or the bitter end. To be at the 'bitter end' meant there was no rope left and the water was too deep to set the anchor.

If something **Goes By The Board** it means it is cast aside, lost in the events. On the old wooden tall ships the 'board' was the side of the boat. Anything falling off a ship and lost forever was regarded as gone past the board, or 'by the board'.

By And Large is a phrase we use as a substitute for 'broadly speaking' or dealing with a subject in general terms rather than in a detailed way. The phrase is a nautical one and dates back to day when ships relied on the wind in their sails. Sailing 'by' means to steer a ship very close to the line of the wind, and sailing 'large' means the wind is on the quarter. This technique made it easier for helmsmen to keep a ship on course during changing winds and in difficult conditions but not in a particularly accurate way, just generally in the right direction. Large ships were assessed on their ability to sail 'by and large'. The phrase was a standard part of the nautical language by 1669 and in wider use by the turn of the following century.

When you have **Had Your Chips** your luck has run out and you are close to failing altogether. Often this is thought to relate to gambling casinos and the gaming chips they use as stake money. This certainly does ring true and can illustrate a situation where a desperate gambler, trying to win back his losses, could be told, 'You have had all your chips now.' But there is an earlier suggestion. An old naval story indicates workers in a dockyard were allowed to take home off-cuts of timber, known as chips, as a perk of the job. It was not uncommon for some men to fall out of favour with the foreman, perhaps for trying to take too many, and to have this privilege removed. In which cases they were told they had 'had all their chips'.

To **Cut And Run** describes pulling rapidly out of a difficult situation and escaping without disadvantage. The phrase was first recorded in 1704 and has a nautical meaning. Hauling a heavy anchor was a difficult task and took many men a considerable time to both free it and raise it back into the sling. Ships coming under attack from the shoreline could suffer considerable damage before the anchor could be dislodged and raised, so it became standard practice to chop the hemp anchor line with an axe and to allow the ship to 'run on the wind'. By 1861 the phrase to 'cut and run' was a standard naval expression.

Davy Jones' Locker is a seafaring expression for the bottom of the ocean and the resting place for drowned sailors. Davy Jones is actually an 18th-century nickname for what sailors thought was the Devil of the sea. It possibly came about thanks to the Caribbean devil spirits known locally as 'duppies' and that other sea legend, Jonah.

Some say the real Davy Jones was a London landlord who would be paid to supply drunk customers to the king's press-gangers, but the more likely explanation is the corruption of the words 'Devil Jonah'. The idea suggested by some that the real Davy Jones was a pirate terrorising the Indian Ocean during the 1600s is hard to substantiate because, if true, then he was not well known enough to have achieved such lasting notoriety. Either way, traditionally an evil sailor's

5

spirit was said to have rested in Davy Jones' locker while the soul of a good man went to Fiddlers Green. The expression has been in use upon the high seas since at least 1751.

Dead In The Water means an idea or scheme has no momentum and no chance of success. This is a nautical expression, dating back to the days of the sailing ships. On a windless day, with nothing to propel the vessel, a boat sitting motionless in the sea was known as 'dead in the water', going nowhere.

To be **At A Loose End** describes a time when we would normally be sitting around with nothing to do. We go back to the old tall ships to define this phrase. Any ship using sails would have thousands of ropes making up the rigging. Each of these lengths would need to be bound tight at both ends to prevent them from unravelling, which would be disastrous during a storm. When the ship's captain found seamen sitting around with nothing to do, he would usually assign them mundane labour such as checking the rigging for loose ends, and re-binding them. Therefore, idle men would find usually themselves 'at a loose end'.

On The Fiddle has nothing at all to do with the previous saying. Instead it implies someone is involved in something not entirely within the rules, and perhaps gaining more than they should be. This is a nautical saying and associated directly with the square ship plate (see **Square Meal**). Those square plates had a raised rim (as did the tables), which prevented food falling off in high seas and these rims were called 'fiddles'. Crew would become suspicious of a fellow sailor with so much food it piled against the rims and they became known as 'on the fiddle' (taking or being given more than they should).

First Rate means something is the best available, near perfect or as good as you can get. From the time Henry VIII began organising the English Navy in the 16th century, war ships were rated on a scale of one to six (a grading that lasted more than 300 years). Then, as now, size mattered and the smallest ships were given a sixth rating, while the largest and best armed were regarded as first rate. Therefore, the best ships to command or crew were known as the 'first rate' vessels, a term that became synonymous with the best of anything.

To **Flog A Dead Horse** is to waste time and energy on a situation that will clearly have a negative outcome. Far out to sea, the Horse Latitudes can be found 30 degrees either side of the Equator, where the subsiding dry air and high pressure results in weak winds. According to naval legend, the area was so called because the tall sail ships, relying on strong winds, always slowed considerably or even stalled altogether. Often it took months to pass through the Horse Latitudes, by which time sailors had worked off what was known as the 'Dead Horse' – the advance wages they had received when signing on. As seamen were paid by the day, the slow passage was to their benefit and there was no incentive to expend much effort in the Horse Latitudes as they worked off their advance wages. Therefore this period of months in the painfully slow mid-ocean became known as 'flogging the dead horse'.

When somebody **Passes With Flying Colours** they have achieved something with distinction, or been successful in a difficult task. The earliest known reference dates back to 1706 and the English Navy, whose term for flag was 'colours'. Victorious and sailing back into London, fleets would demonstrate their success at battle by keeping the battle flags high on the mast and word would soon spread that the Navy had passed by 'with its colours flying', a sure sign of victory.

To feel **Groggy** means to feel generally run down and unwell, often as the result of drinking too much. In 1740 Admiral Vernon, the commander in chief of the West Indies, replaced the neat rum which was then issued to all sailors twice daily, with a watered-down version. The Admiral was a well-known figure and had the nickname 'Old Grog' because of his trademark Grogam coat (a rough mixture of mohair and silk). Thomas Trotter, a sailor on board the *Berwick*, wrote the following passage in 1781:

A mighty bowl on deck he drew
And filled it to the brink
Such drank the *Burford*'s gallant crew
And such the gods shall drink
The sacred robe which Vernon wore
Was drenched within the same
And hence his virtues guard our shore
And Grog drives its name

According to The *Guardian's Notes & Queries, Series I*, the unhappy sailors of the fleet soon began calling the new watered-down ration 'Grog' and as a natural progression drunk sailors were considered 'groggy'.

Making money **Hand Over Fist** alludes to the practice of making steady financial gain, and usually pretty quickly. Back in the 18th century the term was originally 'hand over hand' and was a nautical term meaning 'to make fast and steady progress up a rope'. Later modified to 'hand over fist', alluding to a flat hand passing over the fist gripping the rope, the phrase widened to describe any steady progress in the forward direction, never backwards, such as a boat race. By the late 19th century the financial markets, where often the largest sums could be made out of industrial shipping, had adopted the expression.

Something that is **Hard And Fast** is adhered to without question or argument. Usually it is a rule of some sort. This is a nautical phrase and is the term used to describe a ship that has run aground and is firmly beached on the land. A ship that was hard and fast was not going anywhere in a hurry.

William Henry Smyth's dictionary of nautical phrases, *The Sailor's Workbook*, first published in 1867, defines it like this: 'Hard and Fast: Said of a ship on the shore.'

The expression to be **Left High And Dry** describes being stranded in a situation without support or resource. It's quite simply a nautical phrase, in use from the early 1800s (around the time of the Battle of Trafalgar in 1805), and used to describe a ship left grounded and vulnerable as the tides goes out. A ship's captain who had been left 'high and dry' could do nothing to resolve his situation until the tide returned and refloated his boat. In the meantime the ship was exposed and vulnerable.

To be **Put Through The Hoop** means to be punished or chastised for a wrongdoing. This is a nautical phrase related to the ancient marine custom of 'running the hoop'. The punishment comprised four or more convicted sailors being stripped to the waist, and having their left hands tied to an iron hoop. In the other hand each would hold a length of rope known as a nettle. The bosun would then hit one sailor with a cat o'

11

nine tales and he in turn would have to hit the man in front of him. Being put 'through the ordeal of the hoop' later became shortened to the phrase we know today. Originally, it was a form of horseplay when the ship was in calm waters, but as each blow landed the angry recipient would land a harder blow on the man in turn. As it went on the blows became harder, leading to its effectiveness more as a punishment rather than a game.

Telling a person to **Shake A Leg** means encouraging them to get on with a task. In recent centuries the phrase was well used in public school dormitories, prisons and other institutions where people sleeping in communal rooms would be ordered out of bed at dawn every day. The origin of the saying dates back to the time when civilian women were first allowed on board a ship. At that time the bosun's mate would traditionally rouse the sailors with the cry 'Shake a leg or a purser's stocking.' When a stocking-clad female leg appeared the lady was allowed to stay in her bunk until the men were all up and departed. This was an obvious attempt to preserve her modesty while dressing, but it would seem fair to suggest that a lady on board a ship full of 18th-century sailors may not have had much modesty left worth preserving.

When a person **Splices The Mainbrace**, they are celebrating the successful outcome of an event. The phrase is another dating back to the days of the tall ships that relied upon the wind in their sails. During heavy seas the bosun granted extra rum rations to the sailors who undertook the dangerous duty of climbing the highest rigging, known as the mainbrace. Such sailors were able to celebrate a little more than the others who were given more menial tasks to perform.

Money For Old Rope is simple to explain. In days long gone, when the tall ships returned to their ports, some sailors were allowed to claim old rigging damaged during the voyage. Although of no use to the ships needing long undamaged lines for their sails, parts would still be in good condition and sought after by local traders. Sailors profited by selling it on and, as no effort was required on their part (it was regarded as a perk amongst senior shipmen), some jealousy occurred. The chosen few were criticised for making 'money out of old rope'. These days estate agents have replaced favoured crewmen.

When it is cold enough to **Freeze The Balls Off A Brass Monkey**, we really had better wrap up warm. But who ever heard of such a thing? Old nautical records provide the answer. The guns on 18th-century men-of-war ships needed gun-powder to fire them, and this was stored in a different part of the ship for safety reasons. Young boys, usually orphans, who were small enough to slip through tight spaces, carried this powder along tiny passages and galleys. Because of their agility the lads became known as 'powder monkeys' and by association the brass trays used to hold the cannonballs became known as the brass monkeys. These trays had 16 cannonball-sized indentations that would form the base of a cannonball pyramid. Brass was used because the balls would not stick to or rust on brass as they did with iron, but the drawback was that brass contracts much faster in cold weather than iron. This meant that on severely cold days the indentations holding the lower level of cannonballs would contract, spilling the pyramid over the deck, hence 'cold enough to freeze the balls off a brass monkey'.

A **Nipper** is an affectionate nickname given to a small child, usually a boy. In sailing terms nippers are the small lines that were 'nipped' to the large ship's anchor warps (cables) to make them easier to handle. The job of attaching the lines was a task given to the young cabin boys in a crew, the nippers.

When something is **In The Offing** it is considered to be likely to happen, possibly imminently. The origin of this saying can be found on the high seas in the 17th century. 'Offing' was nautical slang for 'offshore' and a ship approaching a port or coastline, close enough to be seen from land, was considered to be 'in the offing'.

To **Plumb The Depths** is to sink as low in another person's estimation as it is possible to do – to have let yourself, or another person, down in spectacular fashion. This is a nautical term and a plummet (or plumb) was a piece of lead attached to a line used for measuring the depth of the water beneath a ship's hull. Without the aid of modern navigational equipment, sailors of old would rely on this simple method to avoid running aground, especially around the coastlines. The sailor who plumbed the depths literally had to sink the plummet as low as he possibly could. See also **Swing The Lead**.

To **Push The Boat Out** is used to describe a large celebration or expense. This is obviously a nautical expression and relates to the large parties and celebrations sailors would have before setting out on long voyages. A 'pushing the boat out' celebration was always a popular one to attend.

When we look out of the window and it is **Raining Cats And Dogs**, it is too wet to go out. There are several suggestions for the origin of this phrase, one alluding to a famous occasion when it actually rained frogs. Apparently many were lifted into the air during a howling gale and then dropped to the ground around startled pedestrians. Cockney rhyming slang then substituted 'cats and dogs' for 'frogs'.

But I prefer the ancient nautical myth, which led sailors to believe that cats had some sort of influence over storms. According to the Vikings dogs were also a symbol of storms and they always appear in illustrations and descriptions of their own Norse god of storms. (Odin, father of

Thor, was the god of thunder and is described as an old bearded man with one eye who wore a cloak and wide-brimmed hat. Many claim he was the inspiration for JRR Tolkien's character Gandalf in *The Lord Of The Rings*.) Because of this connection, ancient mariners believed that when it rained it was the cats who caused it, and when the gales appeared they were brought by the dogs, leading to the phrase 'raining cats and dogs'.

The phrase first appeared in literature in 1738 when Jonathan Swift wrote in his book *A Complete Collection Of Polite And Ingenious Conversation*, 'I know Sir John will go, though he was sure it would rain cats and dogs.' In 1653 Richard Broome wrote in his play *City Wit*, 'It shall rain dogs and polecats,' suggesting he too alluded to the old nautical tales.

You Scratch My Back And I'll Scratch Yours is a saying with its origins in the English Navy. These days we use it to suggest two people will do each other a favour, or look out for each other so that both parties benefit from one another's actions. During the 17th and 18th centuries the English Navy was traditionally brutal and punishments for disobedience or absenteeism were unimaginably harsh. It was common for a crewmember to be tied to a mast after being sentenced to a dozen lashes, with a 'cat o' nine tails', for minor offences such as being drunk. A 'cat' was nine lengths of thin knotted ship rope bound at one end into a handle. These punishments were usually carried out in full view of the crew, by one of the victim's crewmates. But it was also likely that the crewmate would himself be a victim of the cat o' nine tails at some stage on a voyage, so would be lenient with his victim by applying only light stokes and merely 'scratching' his back. He himself would then receive equally lenient treatment by another shipmate if and when he was on the receiving end.

When you find a person **Three Sheets To The Wind** they are roaring drunk and capable of very little. There are two suggested origins for this phrase. The first is that a windmill with only three sails (sheets) would rotate badly and wobble like a drunk. But the second is far more likely, especially as, like so many phrases, it has a nautical origin. The sails of a tall ship were controlled by rope (the rigging) and these ropes were – and still are – called 'sheets'. Two sheets controlled each sail and the story is that if one of the sheets wasn't properly handled, then the other three (of the two sails) would be 'to the wind'. The boat would then be blown about from side to side and not under full control, much like a drunk trying to navigate his way home.

Shipshape And Bristol Fashion is used to say that everything is neat, tidy and in good order. In the days before Liverpool became a major English port, Bristol was the premier western port from which most ships would embark on transatlantic voyages. It was also a naval port and prided itself on its reputation for efficiency and neatly packed cargoes. The traditional high standards of ships leaving Bristol lead to the phrase passing into the English language.

To **Sling Your Hook** is often used as a 'polite' instruction for somebody to go away. There are several possibilities for this, some referring to the hooks miners or dockers hung their day clothes on during a shift. But the earliest reference is again a nautical one with the hook being a ship's anchor and the sling being the cradle it rests in while at sea. To 'sling the hook' meant to be upping anchor and leaving harbour.

Son Of A Gun began as a dismissive, contemptuous remark, although now it has developed into a more friendly expression, often implying shock and disbelief. Back on the high seas, in the days when women were allowed to live on board the ships, unexpected pregnancy was a regular occurrence. The area behind the mid-ship gun, and behind a canvas screen, was usually where the infant was born. If paternity was uncertain, and it isn't hard to imagine this happened more often than not, the child would be entered into the log as the 'son of a gun'.

Another nautical phrase widely used is **Spick And Span**. These days it indicates something that is new, clean and tidy. Back in the ancient shipyards a 'spick' was a nail or tack (a spike) and a 'span' was a wooden chip or shaving. Newly launched ships, with wooden shavings still present and shiny nails, would be regarded as 'all spick and span' – brand new.

A **Square Meal** is used to describe a good, solid dinner. It is a nautical phrase dating back centuries. Old battleships had notoriously poor living conditions and the sailors' diet was equally bad. Breakfast and lunch would rarely be better than bread and water but the last meal of each day would at least include meat and have some substance. Any significant meal eaten on board a ship would be served on large square wooden trays which sailors carried back to their posts. The trays were square in design to enable them to be stored away both easily and securely, hence the phrase 'a square meal'.

These days **Swing The Lead** is a metaphor used to describe somebody who is avoiding work by giving the appearance of toiling, but not actually doing anything. It is a phrase with its origins in naval history. Aboard ship it was the job of a leadsman to calculate the depth of water around a coastline by dropping a lead weight attached to a measuring line at the bow end. As the easiest job on board it was usually given to a sick or injured seaman and many feigned illness in an attempt to secure such light work. The phrase came ashore and is now used to describe anybody making excuses or simply going through the motions.

A **Washout** is a general failure where no trace of any effort has been made. This expression has its origin in the way the old tall ships passed messages to each other. Naval signals would be read and then chalked on to a slate before being passed to the correct authorities. Once the message had been received, the slate would be washed clean so that no traces of the message would be left other than in the correct hands. This was known as a 'washout' and it is easy to see how the phrase spread into wider use on land.

To be **Under The Weather** means to feel unwell and unable to function properly, and is yet another phrase with its origin out at sea. In days gone by when a sailor was ill he would be sent below decks where he could recover. Under the decks and 'under the weather' his condition could begin to improve.

If we are told to **Whistle For It** the inference is that we are highly unlikely to get the result we want. This is another expression dating back to the early sailing ships circumnavigating the world. The belief among some sailors was that when the day was still, and the sails empty, they could summon the wind by whistling for it. Other sailors disagreed and felt whistling was the Devil's music and instead of a gentle wind arriving a fierce storm would appear. This also explains the origin of the phrase 'whistling in the wind'. Often, whistling would bring no change in the weather at all (no surprises there) but it did lead to yet another saying, 'neither a fair wind nor a storm', meaning the action altered nothing at all.

2: MILITARY

All Present And Correct has been a standard military expression for hundreds of years. After the regimental sergeant major had assembled a regiment on the parade ground for inspection, it would be in his interest to carry out his own assessment of his men before calling for the regimental commander with the traditional words: 'All present and correct, sir, and the men are ready for inspection.' These days it can be used to describe anything we are responsible for, and confident about, before it is to be assessed by another.

Once **The Balloon Has Gone Up** you know there is trouble ahead. During the First World War, observation balloons would be sent into the sky at the first suspicion of an enemy attack, in order to monitor distant enemy troop movements. To most this was a sign of impending action. During the Second World War, strong barrage balloons connected to the ground with thick steel cable were raised around English cities. The idea of these was to impede enemy aircraft, which might crash into them in the darkness or clip their wings on the steel cable. Often they also protected cities from enemy missiles, which would hit a balloon and explode before reaching its target. Their success was immeasurable but to city folk the sign of 'the balloon going up' meant an impending air raid. Trouble was indeed ahead.

To have your **Balls To The Wall** is to be pushing the limit of your machine and driving it as hard and fast as possible. No, chaps, it is not what you are thinking. Instead it is an expression used in the world of aviation. On most aircraft, the levels controlling the throttle and the fuel mixture have ball-shaped grips for ease of handling. Pushing both levers as far forward as possible, towards the wall of the cockpit, is necessary for the aircraft to perform at full power.

To **Beat A Hasty Retreat** means to abandon something, to leave quickly and avoid the consequences of remaining in the same position. This term dates back to the time when a marching army would take its orders from the drummer. Positioned next to the commanding officer, the drummer boy would beat the orders to an army on a battlefield. At night time, or during a battle when things were not going well, the drummer would be ordered to beat a 'retreat' and on hearing the signal a fighting army would immediately cease battle and return to company lines as quickly as they could.

To **Bite The Bullet** is to carry out a task against the doer's wishes. It means getting on with something that just 'has to be done'. This phrase has its origins in the British Empire as the Victorians made friends around the world at the point of a gun. At the time of the Indian Mutiny, gun cartridges came in two parts with the missile part being inserted into the base and held in place by grease made of either cow or pork fat. To charge the bullets the two parts had to be bitten apart and the base filled with gunpowder before they could be fired. This task was usually left to

27

low-ranking Hindu soldiers to whom pigs are holy animals, sacred and not to be desecrated. However they were forced, against their wishes, to 'bite the bullet' in times of battle.

To **Chance Your Arm** is to take an uncalculated risk, where the outcome is completely unknown: a blind bet, if you like. There are several suggestions for the origin of this saying, one being that military men, whose rank was displayed in the way of stripes on their sleeves, would take battlefield risks, which could equally lead to promotion or demotion, depending on the outcome.

A better explanation (at least one that is more fun) dates back to Ireland as long ago as 1492. During a feud between two distinguished families, the Kildares and the Ormonds, during which Sir James Butler, the Earl of Ormond, and his family took sanctuary inside St Patrick's Cathedral in Dublin. The Kildares laid siege outside until Gerald Fitzpatrick, the Earl of Kildare, decided the feud had gone too far and attempted a reconciliation. But the Ormonds were suspicious of his offer of peaceful settlement and refused to leave the cathedral. As a desperate measure to prove his good intentions Fitzgerald ordered a hole to be cut into the cathedral door and then thrust his outstretched hand through, putting his arm at the mercy of those inside as it could easily have been cut off. Instead, Butler took his hand and peace was restored. It is not known if that is actually the origin of the phrase, but it should be.

To be **Sent To Coventry** is to become a social outcast and be ignored by everybody. But why Coventry? During the English Civil War in the mid-1600s Coventry was a strong Parliamentarian town, and Royalist soldiers, captured during the early battles in the Midlands, would be sent to nearby Coventry where they could be certain of a frosty reception. Long before the days of prison camps soldiers loyal to the King could only wander around town looking for food or work but locals would refuse to speak with them, and would even turn their backs and ignore their presence completely. Back then the only entertainment to be found was in local inns but Royalists were barred. Coventry was clearly no place for them but, short of walking back to London, and starving on the way, there was little option but to stay and scavenge. In some cases Royalist soldiers who were deemed useless or not quite committed to the cause would also be garrisoned near Coventry, assuring them of a miserable posting by way of punishment. The idea was that, as no loyalist wanted to be sent to Coventry, they might show more commitment to the King in battle and avoid the posting.

To be **Drummed Out** is to be unceremoniously driven out from a place. It is a military expression relating to the long since outmoded practice of publicly removing disgraced soldiers from their regiments. Such occasions involved the offender being marched from a barracks in front of the assembled regiment to the sound of a single, sombre drum beat. In 1766 Thomas Amory used the descriptive line in his extravagant book, which many believed to actually be his autobiography, *The Life of John Buncle*: 'They all ought to be drummed out of society altogether.' These days nobody uses drums any more, but many are still 'drummed out' of clubs and societies against their will.

A **Feather In Your Cap** means you have done something well and it has been duly noted, although not rewarded by any tangible means other than by having a 'feather placed in your cap'. Its origin seems easy to explain. Any Indian brave fighting for his tribe in America, who killed an enemy, was rewarded by having a feather placed in his head-dress. The most prolific braves would have a headband full of feathers. However, four hundred years prior to this, in medieval England, battlefield bravery was rewarded in a similar way. Knights who had shown great courage were also afforded plumes to wear in their helmets. The Black Prince, 16-year-old Prince Edward, the Prince of Wales of his day, showed such courage at the Battle of Crecy in 1346 (the first great battle of the Hundred Years War) he was awarded the crest of one of his defeated enemies, John of Bohemia. That crest, of three ostrich feathers, remains the crest of the Prince of Wales to this day.

The phrase **Pull Your Finger Out** is associated these days with encouraging someone to get a move on, or hurry up and complete a task more quickly. Like so many English phrases it has a military or naval origin. Loaded cannons would have gun-powder poured into a small ignition hole and held in place with a wooden plug. But in times of battle, when speed was of the essence, the powder would be pushed in and then held in place by a gun crewmember using his finger. Impatient artillerymen, anxious to fire their cannons at the enemy, would shout at the crewmember to 'pull his finger out' so that the gun could be fired. It has not been recorded how many digits were lost on the battlefields.

Flash In The Pan is used to describe something or somebody making a great impression at the outset but ultimately failing to deliver any real result. Of military origin the phrase emerged during the use of early flintlock muskets. Sometimes gunpowder would ignite with a flash in the lock-pan but the main charge failed to light, meaning the shot in the barrel did not discharge, so no harm could come to man nor beast that time round. It was a 'flash in the pan' and the expression was in regular use by 1741.

To **Throw Down The Gauntlet** is to lay a challenge, originally of combat but latterly to any form of contest. A gauntlet is a medieval armoured glove, forming part of a knight's suit of armour. Traditionally a knight would challenge another to a duel by throwing down his gauntlet. If his opponent picked it up it meant he was accepting the challenge and battle would begin. **Taking Up The Gauntlet** has since been a phrase used for accepting a challenge. The Swedish word 'gantlope' (see **Run The Gauntlet**) was anglicised to 'gauntlet' as a result of this tradition, but 'running the gauntlet' and 'throwing down the gauntlet' are not otherwise connected.

Hanging Fire is often used to describe a pause before beginning a task. Sixteenth-century muskets were always slow to fire their charge due to the delay between lighting the gunpowder in the touch-hole and detonation. This was known at the time as 'hang-fire' and the expression was soon used to describe any person delaying or slow to take action.

To Be Hoisted By One's Own Petard means to become a victim of your own deceit, or caught in your own trap. In medieval times a petard was a thick iron container which was filled with gunpowder and set against medieval gates, barricades and bridges. The wicks, however, were unreliable and often detonated the gunpowder immediately, blowing up the engineer in the process. In which case he was 'hoisted (blown up) by his own petard (container of gunpowder)'.

A **Last Ditch Attempt (or Tackle)** is an expression derived from a rousing speech by King William III during the late 17th century, when he called for all Englishmen to 'fight and die in the last ditch' to defend their country.

The expression **Lions Led By Donkeys** is one that can be used to describe any group of capable people being led by inferior officers. This could be said of some teams, unions or businesses. It is generally thought to be an expression emerging from the First World War when millions of fine young men were sent to their deaths thanks to the ineptitude of our generals and warmongers of the day (see also **Over The Top**).

Alan Clark, the late Conservative MP and author, wrote an account of the war entitled *The Donkeys* (1961) that alluded to the image and helped to make it a well-known expression. It was a revisionist account of British involvement in the Great War that annoyed the Army but was very popular with the public. Clark attributes the phrase to a German soldier called Max Hoffman, a brilliant strategist and the architect of the crushing victory by the German Army over the Russians at Tannenberg in August 1914. But in 1871 Francisque Sarcey (1827–1899) had written of the French Army in his book *Paris During the Siege* (1871): 'You are lions led by packasses.'

When a person is considered **Over The Top** it means their behaviour is excessive to say the least. During the First World War, German and Allied troops became engaged in trench warfare, which meant hundreds of thousands of soldiers had to live in trenches in the ground for years on end. Sometimes a military genius would decide to send young British men over the trench wall, hundreds at a time. The order given was always 'Over the top lads and the best of luck' although the latter part was quickly dropped as it became all too obvious that as most were slaughtered by enemy machine guns within seconds, they needed far more than luck to survive. It has been recorded that many young German troopers would be in tears at such carnage and had to be forced to fire by having a pistol held to their heads by their commanding officers.

Very little was gained by this 'over the top' tactic: during the first five months of the war only a handful of yards were won at a cost of tens of thousands of lives on both sides. Those few yards were then lost again: complete madness. That is the source of the expression, which has been widened over the years to include anything outrageous or excessive, sometimes dangerous and often stupid.

To **Pass Muster** is to qualify to a particular standard. In use since approximately 1571, it is a military expression. A 'muster' is another term for bringing troops together for an inspection, so to pass an inspection meant to have passed muster. This is also how we come about the expression to **Muster Up The Courage**.

To take someone **Down A Peg Or Two** means to reduce their status among their peers. It is possible the origin of this phrase is found at sea, and the peg used to fly a ship's colours. The lower the peg, the less impressive the achievement. But there is also a reference dating as far back as the 10th century and King Edred's anger at the amount that his army was drinking. Aware that he needed his soldiers sober for the great battles against the

Vikings, Edred ordered pegs to be put into the side of ale barrels and no man was allowed to drink below the level of the peg in a single sitting. But as soon as this rule was applied soldiers would drink from other people's kegs and take them down a 'peg or two'.

The **Rank And File** are the majority of a group of people, perhaps the workforce of a company or members of a society or union. This is a military expression, emerging from the parade ground. Soldiers lined up for inspection standing shoulder to shoulder are in a formation known as a rank, or the ranks. However, soldiers lined up behind each other are arranged in a file. So, a parade square full of soldiers would be arranged as rank and file.

To **Rise and Shine** is to get up and prepare for the day ahead. It is thought by some to describe washing or shaving, but it is an old military phrase, perhaps originating in America, where soldiers are instructed to rise at dawn, polish their boots and equipment before heading to the parade ground. Apparently the morning call 'Wakey, wakey, rise and shine!' is still traditionally used throughout many regiments.

3: LITERATURE

All Hell Broke Loose is a phrase used to explain complete and uncontrollable mayhem. This expression was an invention of the popular 17th-century writer John Milton whose epic poem, *Paradise Lost*, was published in ten volumes in 1667. Regarded by many academics and critics as one of the greatest poems ever written, it tells the biblical tale of how Adam and Eve fell from favour with an original use of language that was pioneering in its day. In one section, as Gabriel cast Satan from the Garden of Eden, he asks why the Devil had travelled alone: 'Wherefore with thee, came not and all hell broke loose?'

An **Angry Young Man** is something of a rebel who is usually at odds with the established authority. The term was first applied to John Osborne, the playwright responsible for many of the best productions throughout the 1950s and 1960s. The best known of these was *Look Back in Anger* (the inspiration behind the Oasis song of a similar title) that was first staged in 1956 and drew critical acclaim all round. In 1957 George Fearon wrote for the *Daily Telegraph*: 'I had read John Osborne's play. When I met the author I ventured to prophesy that his generation would praise his play while mine would, in general, dislike it... "If this happens," I told him, "you would become known as the Angry Young Man." In fact, we decided there and then that henceforth he was to be known as that.'

Osborne was, no doubt, flattered by the new title but it was not the original use, simply the one that made it well known to the British public. In 1941 Rebecca West, author of *Black Lamb and Grey Falcon*, wrote: 'Their instinct is to brace themselves against any central authority as if it were their enemy. The angry young men run about shouting.'

Dickens was certainly good at inventing phrases. One of them was **Artful Dodger**, which is used to describe somebody involved in crafty or criminal practice. One of Dickens's characters in *Oliver Twist* (1837) was Jack Dawkins, a wily pickpocket and expert member of Fagin's gang of thieves. During the story the author gave Dawkins the nickname 'The Artful Dodger'. Almost immediately the Victorian public adopted the phrase and it was used to describe any crafty rogue.

To be as **Brown As A Berry** is to have a deep brown skin tone. The phrase is usually used to compliment somebody returning from a sunshine holiday. The origin of this particular expression can be traced back as far as what is believed to be the first book ever printed in the English language, Chaucer's *Canterbury Tales*, a collection of stories first published between the years 1387 and 1400. One of them, 'The Monk's Tale', includes the verse:

> He was a lord full fat and in good point;
> His eyen stepe and rolling in his head
> That stemed as a fornice of a led;
> His botes souple, his hors in gret estat,
> Now certainly he was a sayre prelat.
> He was not pale as a forpined gost;
> A fat swan loved he best of any rost;
> His palfrey (horse) was as broune as is a bery.

A person **Clutching At Straws** is making a desperate attempt to have something look, sound or seem to be in better shape than it actually is. It is traceable to the *Dialogue of Comfort Against Tribulation*, published in 1535 and written by Sir Thomas More (1478–1535) whilst awaiting execution for refusing to renounce his faith.

In a fictional account of his own life the writer sets his story in Hungary and uses a dialogue between a young man, Vincent, and his wise old Uncle Anthony as the latter lay on his deathbed. Vincent is terrified of the impending Turkish invasion but the old man calms him and reminds him of the comfort of religion, the overall benefit of suffering and even considers the temptation of suicide. Using the phrase 'a drowning man will clutch at a straw,' More expressed a desire to seek any sort of comfort as his final morning drew nearer.

To have **Cold Feet** indicates a loss of nerve or to have doubts about a particular situation. This phrase has its origins in the gaming world, albeit a fictional one. In 1862 Fritz Reuter, a German author, described a scene in one of his novels during which a poker player fears losing his fortune but does not want to lose face by conceding defeat. Instead he explains to his fellow poker players his feet are too cold and he cannot concentrate. This gives him a chance to leave the table and then slip away from the game. It is not known whether Reuter was drawing on a real life experience (as many novelists do) but his scene certainly appears to be the origin of the phrase.

To **Curry Favour** is a phrase used to describe keeping on the good side of somebody, carrying out acts to keep in favour. The origin of this phrase does not lie in Indian culture, but in the

'Roman de Fauvel', a French satirical poem written in 1310 and popular for centuries. Fauvel was the name of the centaur (half-man, half-horse) who was a beast of great cunning and danger, and to keep on the right side of him sycophants would spend time grooming Fauvel to keep him in a good mood. The art of grooming or dressing a horse is known as 'currying' the animal and therefore those seeking to keep in the centaur's good books could be found 'currying Fauvel'. Over the centuries, and through translation, 'Fauvel' became 'favour'.

A **Dark Horse** is something of an unknown quantity, perhaps somebody whose abilities are not yet fully known but soon will be. In the 16th century the phrase 'to keep something dark' meant keeping something quiet but Benjamin Disraeli created our phrase in his debut novel *The Young Duke*, published in 1831. (At that time Disraeli was only 27 years old and another 37 years away from being Prime Minister.) In his story he describes a horse race in which the two favourites are beaten to the finishing line by an unfancied third. Disraeli wrote, 'a dark horse which never had been thought of rushed past the grandstand in sweeping triumph.' It was common for owners to conceal the potential of their best new horses until the actual day of the race, and almost immediately, throughout the racing world, such animals became known as 'dark horses' regardless of their colour.

Dickens To Pay is used as a threat: 'If you do that again there will be Dickens to pay.' Charles Dickens wasn't a frightening character so as a threat it seems mild to say the least. But the 19th-century novelist has nothing to do with it. As long ago as the 16th century the word 'Devil' was, in fact, 'Devilkin' and having 'the devilkin to pay' meant a passage straight to Hell for one's misdemeanour. Devilkin was usually pronounced 'Dickens', or at least it was in 1601 when William Shakespeare included the line 'I cannot tell what the Dickens his name was' in his play *The Merry Wives Of Windsor* – more than 200 years before Charles Dickens was born.

Or I Shall Eat My Hat is an expression often used to express supreme confidence of an outcome. For generations men and women alike have offered to eat their hats if they are proved wrong about a prediction and they have the author Charles Dickens to thank for that. In *The Pickwick Papers*, first published in 1836, Dickens included the line: 'If I knew as little of life as that, then I'd eat my hat and swallow the buckle whole.' But there is an earlier example, as King Charles II was once quoted as saying 'or I will eat old Rowley's hat.' Rowley was the name of his favourite horse.

To be **Eaten Out Of House And Home** is another great old English expression that emerged from the inventive mind of William Shakespeare. In *Henry IV Part 2* he wrote for one of his characters, Mistress Quickly, the lines: 'It is more than for some, my lord. It is for all, that is all I have. He hath eaten me out of house and home and he hath put all my substance into that fat belly of his. But I will have some of it out again, or I will ride thee o' nights like the mare.'

We have all experienced people who are somewhat **Economical With The Truth** and immediately realise that some important detail has been left out. In other words, we have been lied to. This is an expression that was first used in Parliament, a place where etiquette demands that nobody is directly accused of lying, during the 1700s. But it became widely used by the public in 1986 during a famous trial involving the UK government and Peter Wright, the author of a controversial book called *Spycatcher* that the government claimed was in breach of the Official Secrets Act. A three-year trial, which the government eventually lost in 1988, was high profile and widely reported with transcripts appearing in the news everyday.

One of them, recording a conversation between the Cabinet Secretary Sir Robert Armstrong and a defence lawyer, was reported like this:

47

Defence Lawyer: What is the difference
 between a misleading impression and a lie?
Armstrong: A lie is a straightforward untruth.
Defence Lawyer: Then what is a misleading
impression, a sort of bent untruth?
Armstrong: As one person has said before, it
is perhaps being economical with the truth.

The newshounds loved it and the soundbite was
widely reported, immediately becoming part of
our regular use of language. Although earlier, in
1796, the author and philosopher Edmund Burke
(1729–1797) wrote: 'Falsehood and delusion are
allowed in no case whatsoever. But, as in the
exercise of all the virtues, there can be an
economy of truth. It is a sort of temperance, by
which a man speaks truth with measure that he
may speak it the longer.' Armstrong may or may
not have been aware of Burke's reference.

To describe somebody as a **Good** or **Bad Egg**
would suggest they were either decent,
dependable and reliable or not. The expression
'bad egg' was first used in 1855 in Samuel A
Hammett's novel *Captain Priest* which included the
phrase, 'In the language of his class the Perfect Bird

48

generally turns out to be a bad egg.' The analogy he draws is with an egg that on the outside may appear fresh, but when the shell is broken it may be rotten inside. At the beginning of the 20th century students began reversing the phrase and describing decent people as a 'good egg'.

The phrase **As Sure As Eggs Is Eggs** is used to describe absolute certainty about something. In fact, it is a simple misquote which has passed into common usage. In formal logic and mathematics the formula 'x is x' is used to describe complete certainty. It is unclear how or when 'x is x' became 'eggs is eggs' but it is known Charles Dickens used the phrase 'eggs is eggs' in *The Pickwick Papers*, published in 1837. Maybe Dickens was joking, or playing on words, or possibly it was a simple mistake that proved amusing enough to be left unchanged.

At One Fell Swoop is used to indicate 'in a single movement' or all at the same time, and conjures up an image of a bird of prey swooping down on its target. It is one of Shakespeare's creations. In the Bard's 1606 play *Macbeth*, the character Macduff, on learning his wife and children have all been killed, cries out, 'What, all my pretty chickens, and their dam, at one fell swoop?' The word 'fell' has been used since then to mean 'evil' or 'deadly'.

Sending someone off with a **Flea In Their Ear** implies they have been told off, and in no uncertain terms. The analogy is that of a dog with a flea in its ear, running around in distress shaking its head. The phrase has been used since 1579 when the popular Elizabethan author John Lyly (Lillie or Lylie) published *Euphues, Or The Anatomy Of Wit*. In it he included the line – 'Ferardo... whispering Philautus in his eare (who stoode as though he had a flea in his eare), desired him to kepe silence', as he described a scene where the lord of the manor rebuked a servant.

The phrase **Going For A Song** is used to indicate that something is cheap and priced well below its true value. The actual song, which describes the origin, is in fact a long poem called 'The Faerie Queene', presented to Queen Elizabeth I by Edmund Spenser. At the time it was regarded as Spenser's most popular work but Lord Burleigh, the Lord High Treasurer, was unimpressed. When he heard the Queen intended to pay Spenser £100 for the work, he famously exclaimed, 'What! All this for a song?' The Queen, much to Burleigh's dismay, insisted the money was handed over. The incident was widely reported and the phrase became English slang, although meaning of low value instead of high. The reason for this was the pennies and small change people would toss to buskers and singers entertaining in the hostelries around old London town.

To Kill The Goose That Lays The Golden Egg is to destroy a source of income, or other benefit, through sheer greed. The origin of this saying can be found in one of Aesop's fables, which was translated into English by William Caxton in 1484. In the story Aesop tells the tale of a peasant who discovered a goose that laid golden eggs. In his excitement, and desire to become instantly wealthy, the hapless peasant immediately cut the goose open in order to retrieve the rest of the hidden fortune, killing it in the process and consequently losing his chance of great wealth. The moral of the fable is to be content and have patience, and to caution against greed.

To **Go The Whole Hog** means to do something thoroughly and completely without reservation. Although this is unlikely to be the origin of the phrase, the first reference to it can be found in William Cowper's 1779 poem 'The Love Of The World; or Hypocrisy Detected'. As Cowper describes Muslim leaders trying to work out which part of the hog was edible, he says, 'But for one piece they thought it hard, from the whole hog to be debarred.'

The passing of the phrase into wider use came from the sales tactics of American meat men. Starting in Virginia, enterprising butchers offered joints of meat for sale by the pound, but anybody buying the whole animal would be charged a much cheaper rate, pound for pound. Buying the whole hog and then sharing it around friends and neighbours soon became standard practice for those looking for good discounts on their meat prices. In 1828 Andrew Jackson often used the phrase 'going the whole hog' in his presidential campaign. The election was notable as being the first involving ordinary Americans and campaign leaders organised rallies, parades, dinners and barbecues in order to win votes. Slogans were also used for the first time and Jackson's 'going the whole hog' (going all the way) became known all over America. Jackson won the election, considered at the time as the dirtiest campaign ever witnessed.

How The Other Half Lives is a friendly phrase alluding to the life styles of the rich. The expression can be traced as far back as 1532 and the French book *Pantagruel* by Rabelais and was in use in England by 1607. Jacob Riis used the phrase as the title of a book in 1890 but somewhere along the line the saying has completely changed its meaning. Originally it was a condescending expression used by the rich to describe the poor, but these days it is a light-hearted expression used by the less fortunate to describe the rich.

Ignorance Is Bliss is used to suggest that lack of knowledge equals lack of concern. Originally the phrase alluded to the innocence of youth described in 1747 by Thomas Gray in his poem 'Ode On A Distant Prospect Of Eton College' in the lines 'Thought would destroy their paradise / No more where ignorance is bliss / Tis folly to be wise'. The context Gray uses for the word ignorance is one of limited knowledge rather than the impoliteness or arrogance the word can also be associated with.

Living in an **Ivory Tower** is a mildly pejorative expression used to describe those who live sheltered lives, away from the harsh realities and problems faced by others. It is of French origin and can be traced back as far as the early 1800s, to a poet named Alfred de Vigny. Alfred led a life of disappointment and in his later years withdrew almost completely from society, while continuing to write. In 1837, in a poem called 'Pensees d'Aout' ('Thoughts of August') written by a critic called Sainte-Beuve, de Vigny's lifestyle was described as isolated, and it was suggested he lived in a secluded 'tour d'ivoire' (an 'ivory tower'). The phrase was then widely used to describe other academics who had the reputation of living in a world away from harsh realities, suggesting they knew little about real life.

A **Jekyll And Hyde** character is a person who has two very different sides to his personality. One side is sweet and loving and the other dark and menacing. *The Strange Case Of Dr Jekyll And Mr Hyde* is a story by Robert Louis Stevenson first published in 1886 to instant acclaim. In the story Stevenson describes a doctor (Jekyll) who discovers a drug enabling him to create a separate personality to express his own evil instincts. He calls his new personality 'Mr Hyde'. As the story unfolds Hyde becomes more and more wicked and eventually Dr Jekyll finds the drug too powerful to overcome and he is unable to return to his natural state of calm and reason, leading to his eventual suicide.

A **Leap Of Faith** or a **Leap In The Dark** is a step into the unknown where an outcome cannot be reliably predicted. It is famously suggested the final words of English philosopher Thomas Hobbes (1588–1679) were, 'Now I am about to take my last voyage, a great leap in the dark.' Almost immediately others picked up his words. In 1697 Sir John Vanbrugh wrote in his play *The Provoked Wife*, 'Now I am for Hobbes' voyage, a great leap in the dark.' Other celebrated writers, such as Disraeli, Defoe and Byron, later quoted Hobbes, although over the years the phrase has developed to mean any general uncertainty, rather than the leap into eternity.

To be in possession of **The Lion's Share** is to have the larger part of something, more than anyone else involved. This phrase is another originating from Aesop's fables. One story tells of a lion and three other animals, all hunting together, who catch and kill a stag for their supper. The meal was divided into four equal parts but, just as the animals are about to tuck in, the lion stops them. He insists the first portion is for him as he is king of the jungle and therefore their ruler. He then claims a second portion for himself on the basis he is the strongest of them all and finally a third because of his infinite courage. The lion then allows the other three animals to share the last portion between them but warns them only to touch it if they dare.

The **Movers and the Shakers** are the powerful and influential members of our society: those who can get things done. The expression has been traced to George Chapman's translation, in 1611, of Homer's *Illiad* which included the line, 'Thou mightie shaker of the earth,' in reference to a great power. However, prior to that, in 1589, William Shakespeare was using the lines, 'Thou eternal mover of the heavens, look with a gentle eye upon this wretch,' in *Henry VI Part 2* when the king beseeches God at Cardinal Beaufort's deathbed. In 1874 the English poet Arthur O'Shaughnessy produced his *Ode* (a sonnet about the power of poetry), which provides the first recorded use of the combined term: 'We are the music makers, and we are the dreamers of dreams... Yet we are the movers and shakers, of the world for ever, it seems.'

Namby Pamby is a phrase used to emphasise weakness and childish manner in an adult. The original Namby Pamby was the poet Ambrose Philips (1674–1749), a fellow of St John's College, Cambridge. Philips had achieved success with both *The Distrest Mother* (1712) and his later adaptation of Racine's *Andromaque*, but his infantile language was ridiculed by the great poets of his day. It was Henry Carey who bestowed on Philips the nickname 'Namby Pamby' because his verses were addressed mainly to babies, and it was quickly adopted as part of the English language.

If something is **Piping Hot** it is extremely hot. The pipes that amplified the sound of the old pipe organs found in cathedrals and large churches would hiss in the same way as water does when it steams. When something was 'pipe hot' it was known to be boiling or steaming. The phrase was first recorded during the 1300s and can be found first in Chaucer's *Canterbury Tales* when he wrote, 'Wafers piping hot out of the gleed'. A wafer is a kind of thin cake, baked between wafer-irons, and 'gleed' is the hot coals of a fire.

Our **Salad Days** are the carefree periods of youth when mortgages, insurance and the taxman have yet to enter our minds. The weekend is for living, our partners still look forward to seeing us and the divorce court is a place for old people. The phrase is a simple one with a simple origin provided, once again, by Shakespeare. In 1606 the Bard wrote the play *Antony And Cleopatra*, which includes the line: 'They were my salad days, when I was green in judgement.'

To be **As Happy As A Sandboy** means you are in a state of joyous contentment. This phrase passed into regular usage courtesy of Charles Dickens. In 1840 Dickens published *The Old Curiosity Shop* which includes an inn called The Jolly Sandboys that displayed a sign outside depicting three drunken sandboys. But what was a sandboy?

Dickens is known to have spent time in Bristol, which is referred to throughout *The Pickwick Papers*, published in 1836. Around that time it is recorded that the town's landlords would spread sand on the floor of their establishments which would soak up any spillage, much in the same way as sawdust would be used in other places. In Bristol the Redcliffe Caves are full of sand and innkeepers would send boys off into the caves to provide them with a regular supply. These youngsters were paid partly in ale and consequently they were usually half-cut (merry or jolly), hence Dickens's inn sign and the origin of our phrase.

To have a **Skeleton In The Cupboard** is to have a shameful secret hidden away. I remember as a small boy asking my mother, after watching a programme about missing siblings, if I had any brothers or sisters I didn't know about. She told me we didn't have any 'skeletons like that in our cupboards', which scared the life out of me as I wondered how many children had been locked up forever in cupboards for being naughty. Until 1832 it was illegal to dissect a human body for the benefit of medical research, but of course many a physician still did, and the skeletons had to be hidden somewhere. It is also true that, after dissections became legal, grave robbers would dig up newly buried corpses and sell them to unscrupulous doctors in an underhand way. This practice was so frowned upon that medical men would try to keep their secrets hidden away in locked cupboards. The phrase was first used in print during an article in *Punch* magazine, written in 1845 by William Thackeray, and has been in common usage ever since. My parents probably still wonder where the keys to all the wardrobes in our house went. I imagine they are still over the fence behind next door's shed.

Sour Grapes is a phrase used to describe someone who is sulking or jealous of not having something that others do have. It stems from a simple and popular fable of Aesop called 'The Fox And The Grapes', in which the fox spends a long time trying to reach a bunch of grapes high on the vine, but eventually fails. The fox then comforts himself by explaining he didn't really want them after all, as they looked sour.

An **Ugly Duckling** is a gaunt and awkward child who grows up to be beautiful. This phrase comes from a fairy tale written by children's author Hans Christian Andersen. It tells the story of a duck that mistakenly nests a swan's egg. When the egg is hatched the startled mother duck cannot understand how she has produced such an awkward, ungainly child, which is notably different from the rest of her brood. The cygnet is ridiculed for its dull appearance and hides away in the tall reeds in shame. However, come the spring, the clumsy cygnet emerges from her hideaway having been transformed into a beautiful swan. Danny Kaye's song 'The Ugly Duckling', which was released in the 1950s, popularised the story all over the world.

4: LANGUAGES

To be **Agog** is to be in a state of bewilderment and anticipation, perhaps staring wide-eyed and fascinated at something taking place in front of you. The root of the phrase lies in the old French expression en gogues, meaning amusement or lightheartedness.

To wait with **Bated Breath** means to be anxiously excited and in suspense. 'Bate' is a 14th-century English word meaning to lessen and reduce or to deprive altogether and is an abbreviation of the word abate. It was first used in literature by William Shakespeare in *The Merchant of Venice* in 1596 to describe a person so tense that they could hardly breathe.

To call someone a **Berk** is generally regarded as a mildly humorous put-down without malice, but the origin of the phrase suggests it was very different to begin with. Berk derives from a simple piece of cockney rhyming slang where anybody referred to as a 'Berkshire Hunt' was on the receiving end of one of the most offensive uses of rhyming slang. 'Berkshire Hunt' was shortened to 'Berk' as a replacement for the original meaning, but these days, berk is not at all linked to its original meaning by those using it.

To go **Berserk** means to be in an uncontrollable state, wild and violent. Norse mythology tells the tale of a warrior who would work himself into a frenzy before going into battle and would cast his weapons aside to fight barehanded. Dressed only in a bearskin coat the warrior was universally feared, as were his 12 sons who each had a fearsome reputation. Their battle dress earned them a nickname. Bear is a 'bern' in old Norse and coat is translated as 'serkr' and from this combination they revelled in their reputation of 'berserkers'. Many Viking warriors emulated their example and the word crossed the North Sea to England during the Viking invasion in 865.

To **Blackmail** somebody is to demand money by threats, usually to expose secrets. This word, or phrase, originated in the Highlands of Scotland in the 1600s. The 'mail' in blackmail is the old Scottish word for rent, usually spelled either 'maill' or 'male', which in turn evolved from the Old Norse word 'mal' meaning agreement or contract. In those days tenants paid their rent in silver coins which used to be known as 'white money' but in the 1600s the Highland clan chiefs began a protection racket, threatening farmers and traders with violence if they didn't pay to be protected from other clans. This informal tax, or additional rent, soon became known as 'black money' or 'black rent', being the opposite of white, and so 'blackmaill' became part of the language as a word used to describe the practice of obtaining money by threat of violence. During the 1900s the art of demanding money not to divulge somebody's secrets was established and the use of the word 'blackmail' extended to describe this.

Blighty is an affectionate old-fashioned term for Britain. This developed during the British Empire campaign in India and is taken from the

Hindi word 'Bilayti', meaning foreigner. Empire soldiers used the term to refer to their homeland and the expression was in regular use by the time of the First World War by soldiers who talked of Britain.

Getting down to **Brass Tacks** means that early discussions are complete and we now need to get to the heart of the matter, the details. Some suggestions point to the origin of this phrase being the American drapery stores, where brass-headed tacks were nailed into the counter and used for measuring out fabric. The idea being that, once the customer had taken time to choose their material, putting it to the 'brass tacks' meant actually getting down to the sale. Another explanation is that the phrase stems from the brass tacks found in furniture, which can only be seen when the item is taken apart for restoration. For the real origin we need to look no further than our good old cockney rhyming slang, in which 'facts' are dubbed 'brass tacks'.

A **Card Shark** is often thought to be an incorrect interpretation of the real phrase, a **Card Sharp**. But, in fact, they are both valid expressions as the word 'sharping' was widely used during the 17th century as a word meaning cheating or swindling, and 'sharking' was an earlier expression used to describe stealing, fraud and general trickery. These examples also provide the origin of phrases such as **loan shark** or **sharp practice**.

Two early examples of the expressions in public use can be found in America during the 19th century, both suggesting a wide awareness at the time. One use is found during a report in the *Daily Northwestern*, a Wisconsin newspaper, in October 1893. The story ran:

> And a few days ago Charles Petrie opened a new gambling house that was soon raided by the city police department. Petrie then became angry and called for all gambling houses to be treated in the same way until every card shark in the city was taken in.

A little earlier an unusual story had appeared in the *Hagerstown Mail* during May 1872, claiming there was a pig known as 'Ugly Ben' who was winning card games by pointing his trotters at cards to indicate how he wanted to play them. The story was headlined A PORCINE CARD SHARP.

But there is evidence of a much earlier use of one of the expressions in a painting by the Italian artist Caravaggio (1571–1610) that is dated between 1594–95. The painting, entitled *The Cardsharps*, can be found hanging at the Kimbell Art Museum in Fort Worth, Texas.

To be given **Carte Blanche** is a well-known expression meaning to be given a free hand to attempt a task, without interruption or influence from others. French in origin, the literal translation is white (or blank) paper. It was initially a military phrase (*charte blanche*) in which the surrendering army would give a blank sheet of paper to the victors so they could outline their terms. An early example appeared in the Spectator in 1712 when Joseph Addison wrote, 'I threw her a Carte Blanche, as our newspapers call it, asking her to write it upon her own terms.' An earlier example can be found in 1707, reprinted in the *Hearne Collection* of 1886, which asks the question, 'Who sent the Chart Blanche to make this peace?'

To **Chop And Change** is to be continually changing plans, for no apparent reason and usually to the frustration of all around you. The word 'chop' is actually an old English word, used widely during the 17th century, meaning to exchange. So the original phrase used to mean nothing more than to exchange and change and perhaps change again. The first printed reference appears in *The Life and Opinions of Tristram Shandy*, by Laurence Sterne (1713–1768): 'Surnames which, in the course of the years, have generally undergone as many chops and changes as their owners.'

Sterne was a popular novelist and Anglican clergyman but was also known to mistreat his wife. Once, when waxing lyrical with the playwright and actor, David Garrick, he said, with great sincerity, 'The husband, who behaves unkindly to his wife, deserves to have his house burnt over his head.' 'If you think so,' said Garrick, 'then I hope your house is well insured.'

In 1811, Francis Grose noted, in his *Dictionary of the Vulgar Tongue*, that to chop and change meant: 'to chop, in the canting sense, means making dispatch or hurrying over in any business.' This suggests the expression means to make changes in a hurry without fully comsidering the consequences.

Cockney rhyming slang is responsible for many phrases, and **A Load Of Cobblers** is another of them. These days 'cobblers' means something said is unbelievable or evident nonsense. It is an extension of 'a load of balls', a phrase widely used for centuries in England. A cobbler's awl is a tool used for making lace holes in shoes or boots. In cockney rhyming slang 'balls' became 'cobblers awls', or cobblers. In the Queen's English it means you are talking **codswallop**.

To be **Cut To The Quick** implies deep and emotional hurt. This is a simple phrase to explain as the Old English word for 'living' is *cwicu*. Back in ancient England to be 'cut to the *cwicu*' meant receiving a deep flesh wound.

Having A Dekko is a common phrase for having a look at something. It is often mistaken for cockney rhyming slang but the phrase for that is 'butcher's hook' ('hook' rhymes with 'look'). In fact, having a 'dekko' was introduced to the English language by troops returning from India in the 1800s, during the Empire-building campaigns. 'Dekko' is the Hindustani word for 'look' (or to see).

To describe a person as having **Gone Doolally** is to suggest they have gone mad. In the late 19th century, as the British Empire dominated the world, the British Army established a military base at Deolali, 100 miles north of Bombay in India. The base had an asylum, into which unstable battle-weary troops would be sent, but it also doubled as a transit camp where soldiers, at the end of their duty tour, would be stationed to await the boat home. But ships only left for Blighty between November and March so some soldiers had months to wait for their transportation. The ensuing drawn-out weeks of heat, exhaustion and boredom often resulted in strange and eccentric behaviour. This behaviour would be explained, on their return to Britain, as the man having 'gone through Deolali'. Doolally was recorded as military slang in 1925. (See also **Basket Case**.)

A **Doss House** is used to describe living accommodation that is basic in the extreme and a **Dosser** is an unkind word used to describe somebody living there or in any other cheap, temporary place. The phrase is traced back to Elizabethan England during the late 16th century when a basic straw bed was known as a 'doss', taken from the French word 'dossel' meaning bundle of hay. Farmers and other landowners would rent out straw beds in barns, or other basic shelters, to the homeless and these places, lined with 'dossels' were known as doss houses.

To **Egg On** is a term used to urge or encourage somebody, usually into doing something foolish or risky. The phrase is almost as old as eggs themselves and its origin can be found in the old Anglo-Saxon language where the word 'eggian' means to spur on, or from the Old Norse word 'eggja', meaning to incite. To 'eggian' a person was to encourage or incite them.

On the face of it, the expression **Fair And Square** would seem more odd than obvious. But during the 15th and 16th centuries the old English word for honest, sincere and reliable was 'square'. So the real expression is 'fair and honest' but the phrase remains in use in its original form. That is also why some would call an apparently law abiding and honest man a square.

To **Run The Gauntlet** means to place one's self at risk of attack from all sides, either physically or verbally. It is of Scandinavian origin. In the 1600s the Swedish military would punish soldiers or sailors by forming two lines of men, each armed with a short length of rope or a baton. The offender was then forced to run down between the lines, while his comrades beat him as hard as they could. The Swedish word for passageway is 'gantlope' and this was later anglicised to 'gauntlet' by the English military, who discovered this form of punishment during the Thirty Year War (1618–48). The practice was abolished in 1813 but remained a method of public school bullying well into the 1900s.

To **Wreak Havoc** means to cause major confusion and destruction. The expression began life as 'Cry Havot' which is the old French expression for 'plunder'. In widespread use by the 13th century, the phrase evolved into Anglo-French as 'Cry Havoc'. During a military campaign the cry of 'havoc', by the generals, was the signal that the battle was won and the pillaging and looting could begin. In 1386 Richard II banned the use of the phrase on pain of death but Shakespeare used the term in several of his plays, which is how it passed over into wider use.

Hob Nobbing with somebody implies keeping their company or associating with them. This expression is the perfect example of how, as the English language progresses, word corruption often occurs. Originally the phrase used was 'hab nab' which was shortened from the Old English word 'habban', meaning 'to have', and 'nabban', meaning 'not to have'. This expression then took on the meaning of 'to give and take' in the context of drinks. But in 1811 the *Oxford English Dictionary* tells us that in the corner of an open fireplace there was usually a small ledge called a hob, which was used to warm cold wine or beer. The table this was then served upon was called a 'nob', suggesting that 'hob and nobbing' was a term for sharing drinks. By 1861 Charles Dickens had used the phrase in his novel *Great Expectations* and it passed over into wider use as a term for associating with someone.

If we are **In Cahoots** we are planning an event in secrecy. An American term, it has developed from the French word 'cahute', meaning 'small hut'. The phrase was used by native Americans to describe the French settlers during the 17th century and has come to mean groups of people colluding with each other unseen in confined spaces.

Keeping Shtoom is a well-known expression for staying quiet, or silent for fear of revealing something that could cause problems or trouble. Its earliest written use can be found as recently as 1958 in Frank Warner's book *Bang to Rights: An Account of Prison Life*. 'I think it is much better to keep shtoom. You can always shtoom up if any screws are earholing.' Warner had spent three years in prison during the 1950s and the expression was already well-known prison slang by that time. Deriving from the German word for silent (or dumb), which is *stumm* (pronounced 'schtumm'), the word became part of prison language during the Second World War when German prisoners would simply repeat the word stumm under interrogation.

To put the **Kibosh** on something usually means it is stopped in its tracks, effectively ended. This sounds like a Jewish word and sure enough its origin can be found in Hebrew, where 'kabash' means to subdue or to bring into subjection.

If you **Lambast** someone, they are on the receiving end of a very severe rebuke or reprimand. Emanating from the Old Norse word 'lamia' meaning 'to make lame', the phrase entered the English language as 'Lam' meaning 'to beat soundly'. 'Baste' is the Old Norse word for 'thrash', or 'flog', and over time the two words have connected to provide the phrase in use today.

To be **At Large** is usually applied to a prisoner who has escaped and is free from custody. It is one of those strange phrases that appear to have no basis in the English language, and indeed it doesn't. The French have the phrase 'prendre la large' which means 'to stand out and be free to move', from which our expression has developed.

When somebody is **Larking About** they are playing around in a silly manner. There is a suggestion that the phrase is linked to skylarks, who frolic around in the sky on summer evenings, but the expression derives from the Middle English word 'Laik' which means to play and the Old English work 'Lac' meaning a contest. By the 18th century the word 'lark' was established as part of the English language meaning 'amusing adventure or escapade'.

To **Use Your Loaf** means to show some common sense and intelligence. The origin for this is simple – 'use your loaf of bread', which is 'head' in cockney rhyming slang.

To be **Left In The Lurch** means you have been left at a disadvantage, usually by someone close to you. There is an old French game of dice called 'lourche', the object of which is to leave your opponent way behind you on the score card. When this happens, the trailing opponent incurs a lourche (a disadvantage). The phrase became anglicised via the card game of cribbage. During the scoring process if a player reaches 51 holes on the cribbage board, before another reaches 31, the trailing player is deemed to have been left in the lurch. It can also be noted that, once a winner has placed his peg in the final hole of the score board, causing the game to be over, he is considered to be **Pegged Out**, a phrase used to described being exhausted, or finished for the time being.

When somebody makes a **Moot Point** they are suggesting something so vague and ambiguous that it is open to debate. 'Moot' derives from a wonderful old Anglo-Saxon word 'gemot' which means 'meeting'. Saxon society was made up of many different assemblies where public issues could be debated. A 'wardmote' was a ward meeting, a 'burgmote' was a town meeting and the grand 'witenagemote' was a meeting of prominent wise men. During the 16th century the moot courts, or the mootings, were established at the Inns of Court in London. This was the place where young law students were able to practise their powers of argument and debate by taking part in hypothetical trials. It is a practice that continues to this day and forms the origin of this phrase.

Mufti Day is a day many school children look forward to as it means they can spend the day in their own choice of clothes, rather than in school uniform. In the work place many companies now also have a 'mufti day' and employees can dress casually for a small donation to charity. The phrase is a military one and originates in the Middle East where British officers and their troops would relax in dressing gowns, smoking caps and slippers. This appearance was similar to that of a costume worn by experts in Muslim law, who are called 'muftis'. The expression returned to Britain with the military and passed into wider use during the 19th century.

When something is **Out Of Kilter** it is unbalanced, uncoordinated and generally not working properly. In Old English the word 'kilter' – or 'kelter' in some dialects – meant either 'condition' or 'order'. The phrase is known to have been in use in England since 1628 and has managed to survive intact for centuries.

A **Phoney** is regarded as fake, not the genuine article. 'Fainne' (pronounced 'fawnya') is a Gaelic word meaning circle or ring. In the 18th century some Irish gold was not regarded as genuine and by 1811 gold rings from that country were known as 'fawney', which became an English slang word meaning fake. During the 1920s imitation gold rings passed on by American confidence tricksters were also regarded as 'fawney', although their accent led to a corruption and the word became 'phoney'.

A **Plum Job** or a **Plum Role** is considered to be one of the best and most important a person can have. During the 1600s the slang term in England for £1,000 was 'plum', in the same way as a 'monkey' is now £500 and a 'score' is £20. Back then £1,000 was a seriously large amount of money but it was the fixed amount some politicians received for certain government roles. This was considered by the average layman to be a vast sum of money for doing very little and these posts became known as 'plum jobs'. It is easy to see how this phrase caught on and is applied to this day to easy or privileged positions, although it is often used in admiration rather than the contempt the expression started with.

Point Blank range means very close to and is usually used in relation to gunfire, as in 'shot at point blank range'. The origin is a military one and stems from the French word 'point blanc' which means centre, or bullseye. It was used to describe the flight of an arrow that flies directly at its target. In other words, you are close enough to the target for no arcing to take place. To tell someone point blank, as in 'I told him point blank the answer was no' also suggests the conversation was held at very close range, face to face.

A **Pommy** or **Pom** (pronounced pomme) is Australian or South African slang for an Englishman. For years Australians have taunted the English with phrases such as 'whingeing pom' and 'useless pommy' – particularly with regards to our cricket and rugby teams when they are not performing well against the Aussies. Those delightful Australians regularly call our sportsmen and sports fans 'pommy bastards'. Former Australian rugby captain David Campese made headlines during the 2003 Rugby World Cup with a similar comment as he allegedly said the 'Poms would win nothing' but win it England did, by beating Australia in the final on their home soil.

The expression arises from the acronym P.O.M.E. meaning 'Prisoner of Mother England', or perhaps P.O.H.M. meaning 'Prisoner of His/Her Majesty'. Either way, it was a name given to those English convicts who were transported to Australia between 1787 and 1868 and who were not natives of that country. So that means if you are not an Aborigine living in Australia then you are a Pommy. And that means you, Mr Campese, your fellow countrymen and all your ancestors – not us still living in England, because none of us are descended from transported criminals.

A **Pundit** is supposed to be an expert on a subject. Every day various pundits appear on television, radio and all over our newspapers providing their opinion on matters from football and politics to cookery and entertainment. India has been a rich source of English idioms since the days of the British Empire and the word pundit is another that can be traced back to those days. In India a 'Pandit' is a Hindu scholar or learned man who is well versed in the law, religion, ancient scriptures and Sanskrit. The word was brought back to Britain during the 19th century and used to describe any expert or authority on just about any subject.

The **Rag, Tag and Bobtail** of society are something of a rabble – the underclass, those we can do nothing for. The BBC used to broadcast a popular children's programme of this name but the origin of the expression can be traced to the 16th century, when the word 'bobtail' was London slang for a villain, scallywag or rascal. Rags were the clothes they wore and a 'tag' was a torn piece of cloth hanging loose from a jacket or shirt. On one occasion in 1659 Samuel Pepys recorded in his diary, 'The dining room was filled with rag, tags and bobtails all dancing, drinking and singing.' Sounds like a good night out.

A **Round Robin** is usually a newsletter or general information pack available to everybody. But it was originally a petition of some sort, originating in France at the time of the peasant revolts during the 17th and 18th centuries. At these times it was never a good idea to petition the king, because the kindly old soul would call in the three or four names at the top of the petition, presumed to be the ring leaders, and cut their heads off. So the revolting peasants devised an ingenious new method of petitioning. 'Rond Ruban' was a length of ribbon fastened to itself, forming a circular ribbon. This way anybody could sign a petition and there would be no way of knowing whose were the first signatures. It didn't do them any good, though, until they finally stormed the Bastille on 14 July 1789 and put an end the reign of the French royal family for good.

These days a round robin can also be used to describe any sporting contest where every player competes against each other before the outcome is determined.

Not A Sausage is a way of describing either something as free of charge or one's own self as being penniless. It is derived from another example of the colourful cockney rhyming slang of London, where sausage and mash was a staple diet between the 17th and 18th centuries. To be without 'sausage and mash' is to be without cash.

To suggest a person is **No Great Shakes** is to imply they are not particularly effective, and not up to a given standard. The word 'shakes' in this context comes from the Old English word 'schakere', which means to boast or brag. This was a phrase used frequently in the 13th century and the phrase 'of no great schakere' meant a person had nothing to boast about. A second widely held belief is that the phrase comes from the game of dice, suggesting a poor player wasn't any good because his 'shakes' were not effective enough.

To be **In A Shambles** is to be in a state of complete disarray. This phrase is usually used as a criticism of a person, group of people or a situation. The word 'shambles' derives from the Old English word 'sceamul' (pronounced 'shamell') which means 'stool' or 'table' as in a butcher's workbench. During the medieval period most towns had certain streets exclusively occupied by a single trade. There would be whole rows of fishmongers, greengrocers and butchers, which were known as 'shambles'. Some old towns such as York still have streets called The Shambles. Street butchers were supplied by the slaughterhouses and such was the mess of blood and animal parts by the butchers' workbenches they too became referred to as 'shambles'. This then became a metaphor for general mess and chaos.

Thick As Thieves is a term used to imply two or more people are on very close, friendly terms with each other, often with a common purpose. It stems from a French phrase 'like thieves at a fair', which describes groups of villains working in close collusion, which then hopped the Channel during the Norman Conquest in 1066. In England the saying was first used by author Thomas Hook in his novel *The Parson's Daughter*, which was published in 1833. Contrary to popular belief, the phrase 'thick as thieves' is not a reference to the intellect of those residing at Her Majesty's Pleasure.

To **Take Umbrage** means to take offence at somebody's remarks or behaviour. The word 'umbrage' has its roots in the Latin word 'umbra' meaning shade (which is also where the word 'umbrella' comes from). In England, 'umbra' was used to describe the shade or shadow cast by a line of trees and came to mean the shadow or shade a person is put under by suspicion or doubt. To be put in such a shadow will give rise to resentment and ill feeling, hence 'taking umbrage'.

Without Batting An Eyelid is a common phrase used to describe a person taking a situation in their stride, without even blinking in surprise. 'Bate' is a long obsolete English word meaning 'to flutter' or 'to beat the wings' as a butterfly might. When a person reacted, to something without showing any signs of surprise (blinking) they were regarded as 'not even bateing an eyelid', which later mutated into the phrase we use today.

To get off **Scot Free** means to have escaped punishment and avoided the consequence of a bad deed. The origin of the phrase is traced to Scandinavia (not Scotland as it would appear) and the word 'scot' meaning 'payment'. Around the

13th century a great municipal tax called 'scot' was imposed on the Scandinavian people. All households were required to pay according to their means but the peasants were exempt. They were known as 'scot-free'. In England the scot tax lasted in some places for hundreds of years, finally petering out during the Westminster electoral reforms in 1836.

It is also known that during the Middle Ages innkeepers would hold a record of a person's drinking on a slate called a scot and to leave an establishment without paying was known as 'going scot free'.

5: THE ANCIENTS: GREEKS AND ROMANS

An **Achilles' Heel** is a perceived weakness in someone or something otherwise considered solid and perhaps infallible. As the ancient Greek legend goes, Thetis dipped her son Achilles into the river Styx with the intention of making his skin armour-like and impenetrable. But she held him by his heel, which remained out of the water and as a result his only vulnerable spot. Achilles grew up to be an invincible soldier but his deadly enemy, Paris, learned of his weakness and killed him during the Trojan War with an arrow shot straight at his heel. Homer told the full story in his *Iliad*.

To **Add Insult To Injury** suggests a second remark or action makes an already bad situation worse by adding another problem. It is suggested the origin of the saying dates back to 25 BC and a book of fables by the Roman writer Phaedrus. In his story 'The Bald Man And The Fly', Phaedrus describes a fly stinging a bald man on the top of his head. Angry at being bitten the man attempts to kill the fly with a hard slap, but the insect sees this coming and jumps off, leaving the man to slap only his head. The fly then insults the man for trying to kill it over a simple insect bite. The bald man had not only received an injury, in the shape of a bite on the top of his head, but also suffered the indignity of making it worse and being insulted by the fly.

To keep something **At Bay**, such as danger or illness, means to fend it off and not be affected by it. In ancient history the bay tree was thought to possess great protective powers, as they never seemed to be struck by lightning. Romans and Greeks would seek shelter under a bay tree during storms and warriors took to wearing bay leaves as a means of protection against both the enemy and thunderstorms in an attempt to keep them 'at bay'.

During the Great Plague of London in 1665 city folk did the same in the hope they would avoid the disease and keep the plague 'at bay'.

To have the **Bit Between Your Teeth** means to go about a task with such enthusiasm and determination that nobody can stop you. This term relates to the metal bar in a horse's mouth attached to the reigns enabling a rider to steer and control the animal. This bar is known as the 'bit' and needs to be positioned at the softer back of the mouth where the horse can feel it. If the bit gets caught further forward, between the teeth, the horse becomes insensitive to a rider's instructions and therefore uncontrollable. The expression dates back to the year 470 BC and Greek culture when Aeschylus remarked, 'You take the bit in your teeth like a new-harnessed colt.'

When somebody is described as a **Real Brick** they are complimented on their reliability and their solid and dependable nature, somebody beyond the call of duty. The ancient Greek legend of the city of Sparta tells a story of its king, Lycurgus, who had failed to build defensive walls around his kingdom, as was the custom of the day. When questioned about this King Lycurgus is said to have pointed to his soldiers and replied, 'But I have a wall, and every man is a brick.'

If we **Burn Our Bridges**, we are putting ourselves in a position from which there is no return, often to our great cost. This phrase can be traced back to the Roman Army, whose generals adopted the practice of burning the bridges their soldiers crossed on their way into battle, removing any thought of retreat from their minds. They also used to **Burn Their Boats** after sea invasions, once again eliminating any idea of withdrawal.

'My **Ears Are Burning**' is a remark made by a person to suggest they are being talked about by others at that moment. Quite often we experience a tingling or slight burning sensation in either ear and the superstitious Romans believed all such things were signals. 'It is acknowledged that the absent feel a presentiment of remarks about themselves by the ringing of their ears' (*Naturalis Historia*, AD 77). As the Romans also firmly believed everything on the left signified evil and on the right implied good, the theory was that the left ear burning suggested evil intent and the right ear praise. Sir Thomas Brown (1605–82) in his book *Extracts From Christian Morals* suggested guardian angels were responsible and they touched the right ear if the talk was favourable and the left if unfavourable.

Eat Your Heart Out is a phrase we use in good humour to taunt another person. The suggestion is that they should be envious of and worried about another's achievement. The saying was a favourite Jewish expression in showbusiness circles during the 20th century but was certainly in use much earlier. Diogenes Laertius credited Pythagoras with saying 'Do not eat your heart' meaning 'Don't waste your life worrying about something.' And that was 2,500 years ago.

To **Fiddle While Rome Burns** is a phrase often used to describe somebody being occupied by small details while a greater disaster is taking place unnoticed. Roman legend has it that in AD 64 Emperor Nero wanted to see what Troy had looked like as it burned to the ground, so he set light to Rome. It was said that he watched the blaze for six days and seven nights while he played his fiddle and enjoyed himself. Nero

93

strongly denied the claims and blamed the disaster on the Christians, who were then ruthlessly persecuted. Historians have confirmed Nero was nowhere near Rome when the fire started, supporting his defence. Instead he was probably out enjoying himself at the School of Charm run by Caligula.

To **Go With The Flow** means not to have a strong opinion and thus follow the majority. Often thought to be of American origin, the phrase in fact predates the Yanks by about 1,600 years. Marcus Aurelius was crowned Emperor of Rome on 7 March 161. His turbulent reign was characterised by war and disaster but also, above all, intellectual thought. Marcus dealt with his turmoil through stoic philosophy and much of this is expressed in his writings *The Meditations*, in which he displays the tension he felt between his position as emperor and his prevailing feeling of overall inadequacy. Much of Marcus's philosophy is based around the flow of thought and the flow of happiness and he concluded that 'all things flow naturally'. Marcus also expressed the opinion it was better to 'go with the flow' rather than try to change the natural course of events.

The phrase **Beware Of Greeks Bearing Gifts** is a friendly warning against trickery and deception. This phrase refers to the most famous Greek gift of all, the Trojan Horse. During the Trojan Wars the Greeks had besieged the city of Troy for over ten years. Finally, as they made plans to leave, they built a huge wooden horse as an offering to the gods and a sign of peace. The horse was left at the gates of Troy and, once the Greeks had withdrawn, the people of Troy opened their gates, for the first time in a decade, to receive the apparently harmless gift. However, as soon as the horse was inside, Greek soldiers poured out of the wooden structure and destroyed the city. Virgil, in the *Aeneid* (II.49) has Laocoon warn the Trojans about accepting the horse, saying, 'I still fear the Greeks, even when they offer us gifts.'

When something **Hangs By A Thread** it means a situation could change in an instant. The phrase alludes to the sword of Damocles that was hung from a ceiling by a single hair. The Roman philosopher Cicero tells the story that in 400 BC Dionysius the Elder, ruler of Syracuse, became tired of one of his courtiers, Damocles, for his slimy bootlicking. To remind the young servile how fortunate his position was, and how tenuous it might be, Dionysius sat Damocles beneath the sword during a banquet. Not only did the sword 'hang by a thread' but so did Damocles's life. Cicero used the incident to illustrate that he understood how tenuous his own privileged position was.

When somebody claims they **Don't Give A Jot** they are implying they care nothing at all about a circumstance. The phrase is thousands of years old and is exactly the same as the expression **I Don't Give One Iota**. The origins for both can be found in the early Greek language. A jot is the letter 'iota' which is the smallest in the Greek alphabet. It was used at the time to imply 'the least of anything'.

A situation that is in the **Lap Of The Gods** is one where the outcome is unclear and cannot be influenced in any meaningful way. Early suggestions for the origin of this saying predictably pointed to the practice in many cultures of leaving gifts with statues of gods in the hope of answered prayers. But Homer's *Iliad* probably holds the answer. In the story Patrocolos, a friend of Achilles, is killed by the Trojans who then intended to parade his severed head to demoralise their opponents. With the battle in the balance, and the outcome uncertain, Automedon declared, 'These things lie on the knees of the gods.' On hearing this Achilles returned and led an unexpected rout of the Trojans, confirming to all that the gods were well and truly on the side of the famous warrior.

To **Lick Something Into Shape** means to mould something (or someone) to suit a particular task or situation. Bizarrely, some races used to believe that some animals, particularly bears, gave birth to formless offspring and then licked them into the shape of their breed. This is possibly because many animal offspring are born covered in a thick afterbirth, sometimes making them almost unrecognisable until a mother has cleaned it off. Around AD 150 Aulus Gellius wrote, 'For he said that as the bear brought forth her young formless and misshapen, by licking gave it form and shape.' And we thought the Romans were knowledgeable.

Like Rats Leaving A Sinking Ship is a derogatory phrase used to describe people with no loyalty or faith – perhaps a politician rapidly losing favour or employees leaving a company believing it to be going under. The original expression dates as far back as the first century AD and the works of Pliny, the Roman philosopher. He believed mice had such acute hearing they could detect, from the creaking and groaning of houses' wooden structures, when one was about to collapse. But William Shakespeare provided the more modern version when he wrote in *The Tempest*: 'It was a rotten carcass of a boat and the rats have instinctively left.'

Lily Livered is a term used for cowards, or cowardly behaviour. The ancient Greeks had the custom of sacrificing an animal on the eve of each battle and the animal's liver was considered a major omen. If it was red and full of blood all the signs were positive but, if the liver was pale and lily-coloured, it was thought to signify bad tidings. The Greeks also believed the liver of a cowardly person was pale and lily-coloured.

When a person is described as **Mealy Mouthed** the implication is they are unwilling to speak plainly or openly about something, in case what they have to say offends. It is often used as a derogatory term for somebody who is trying to please others. Its origin can be found as a phonetic adaptation from the ancient Greek 'melimuthos' which means, literally, 'honey speak'.

To make a **Mountain Out Of A Molehill** means to exaggerate something out of all proportion. The original phrase was 'to make an elephant out of a fly' and dates back to the ancient Greek satirist Lucian, who lived in AD 2. But in 1548 Nicholas Udall wrote *Paraphrase Of Erasmus* which includes the line: 'Sophists of Greece could, through their copiousness, make an elephant of a fly and a mountain of a molehill.' The original expression has long been forgotten but Udall's replacement remains a commonly used phrase.

A person not likely to **Rest On Their Laurels** continues to make an effort even after a positive result has been achieved. A writer, for example, after being lucky enough to have a best-selling book, might go straight back to work in an attempt to repeat his success, rather than relax and enjoy his achievements.

During the ancient Pythian Games held at Delphi in Greece, a custom began of presenting the winners of events with victory wreaths made out of bay laurel leaves. This practice soon became tradition and was repeated at sporting events all over the world, including, more famously, the Olympic Games. A number of laurel wreaths may have been presented to any successful athlete and, naturally, there may have been a time when he could decide his work had been done for the day, make a seat out of his laurels and sit back to enjoy the rest of the games.

Rome Wasn't Built In A Day is a phrase used to provide encouragement and patience when something is taking longer to achieve than expected. It is an old Latin proverb dating back to around the time the once greatest city in the world was built. According to legend, the architect Romulus and his twin brother Remus founded Rome in 753 BC. For research purposes I have just come back from Rome and can confirm it certainly was not built in a day. In fact it looks like they are still building it.

The **Rule Of Thumb** is a rough estimate based on experience rather than formal calculation. The expression has been in wide use since the late 1600s and there are several suggestions for its origin. One of them emanates from the ale-makers where, in the days before accurate thermometers were available, the brewer would test the temperature of fermenting beers by dipping his thumb in. If this was the phrase's origin one would expect to find pubs called The Brewer's Thumb, but I can find none.

Another suggestion dates back to the Middle Ages when it was legal for a man to beat his wife with a cane no thicker than his thumb. Evidence of this comes to light in the *Biographical Dictionary Of The Judges Of England* written by Edward Foss in 1864. In the text Foss suggests that a 'husband may beat his wife, so that the stick with which he administers the castigation is not thicker than his thumb'. It should also have been possible for a wife to beat the man who put that law on the statute book with a stick no thicker than he was. Instead we go back to the Romans who used the tip of the thumb (from the knuckle upward) as a unit of measurement, as any thumb would fit roughly 12 times into the next unit of measurement, a foot. There is definitely a connection here, as the French word for inches is 'pouces' which translates as 'thumb' and that remained a standard unit of measurement until metrification. The Roman bricklayers used their thumbs to estimate measurements and the phrase has been in standard use ever since.

If a person is **Not Worth His Salt** they are regarded as not very good at their job and not worth the wages. During the days of the Roman Empire salt was an expensive commodity and soldiers were actually paid partly in salt, which they carried in leather pouches. This payment was known as 'salarium', from the Latin word 'sal', meaning salt. The modern word for wages, 'salary', also originates from this source.

The origin of the phrase **Taken With A Pinch Of Salt** goes as far back as AD 77 and the Latin *Addito Salis Grano* written by Pliny the Elder. The elderly Pliny had discovered the story of King Mithridates VI, who once ruled Pontus and built up his immunity to poisoning by fasting and then taking regular doses of poison with a single grain of salt in an effort to make it more palatable.

Scallywag is a word used particularly around the Liverpool area, to describe a boisterous, energetic and disruptive young male who has little regard for authority. The word started life as 'scurryvag', which comes from the Latin phrase 'scurra vagus' meaning 'wandering fool'. In London the word 'scurryvag' was used to describe a scurrilous vagrant (a merging of the two words) which later became scallywag thanks to the Liverpool accent.

To **Spill The Beans** is a widely used term for giving away a secret. A tradition that began in ancient Greece for electing a new member to a private club was to give each existing member a white and brown bean with which to cast their votes. The white bean was a yes vote and the brown meant an objection. The beans were then secretly placed in a jar and the prospective member would never know how many people voted either for or against him. Unless, that is, the jar was knocked over and the beans spilled. Then the club members' secret would be out.

Spondulics is a slang word for money. According to the *Oxford English Dictionary* it is a word of 'fanciful origin' but my Greek friends have

103

managed to trace it back to their ancient language and the word 'spondulikos', which derives from 'spondulos', a type of seashell. Apparently this shell was once used as a currency and is very likely to have been the origin of our slang phrase. In addition, the Greek word for spine, or vertebrae, is 'spondylo' and a stack of coins could resemble a spine. This suggestion is supported by John Mitchell in his book *A Manual Of The Art Of Prose Composition*, first published in 1867, in which he lists 'spondulics' as a 'coin pile, ready for counting'.

Leaving **No Stone Unturned** is a phrase we use to describe having made all possible efforts to complete a task. After the Greeks defeated the Persians at the battle of Plataea in 477 BC, Polycrates set about finding the treasure he thought had been left in the tent of the Persian general Mardonius. After searching everywhere he turned to the oracle at Delphi who advised him to 'move every stone' in his search. Polycrates took that advice and subsequently found the treasure. The phrase soon became popular and only a few years later, in 410 BC, Aristophanes called it 'that old proverb'. At nearly

2,500 years old, 'no stone unturned' may even be our oldest idiom.

To **Swear On Your Testicles** (stop laughing at the back) is an old phrase dating back to the Romans and their apparent courtroom practice of swearing the truth of a statement on their testicles. In fact, there is some truth in this, as the Latin word for a witness is *testis*, which is taken from the old Indo-European word for the number three. The Romans regarded an impartial witness, who could look at events in an objective way, as a third party, which is how testis developed as the word for witness. But they did also use the word 'testis' as a witness to a man's virility, which is how the word testicle also evolved and how the two are connected. But, when a Roman was swearing on his testicles, he was actually swearing on his witness. No doubt this has had Latin students sniggering for generations.

To **Thread Your Way** through a crowd is an old English phrase dating back to the mid-1500s. Back then the good and the great would entertain themselves for hours in a new modern puzzle called mazes. However, many people soon realised it was just as hard to find their way out of a maze as it was to reach the centre. Some adopted the practice of taking a clew (a cheap yarn or thread) and fixing one end at the beginning, enabling them to find their way back out again and that lead to the term 'threading your way through'. But this wasn't a new trick, even in the 1500s. It was borrowed from the ancient Greek myth in which Theseus finds his way back out of the Minotaur's labyrinth after slaying the beast, by using a 'clew' of thread. A slight variation of the word 'clew' led to 'clue' becoming used in modern English language as the term for anything helping to unravel puzzles or mysteries. The word 'maze' itself stems from the word 'amazing', which was used to describe the popular new game.

When somebody is described as **Two Faced** it is suggested they are hypocritical, prepared to share one opinion with a person and then a conflicting viewpoint with another. The inference is they have a separate face for each contrary opinion. Janus was a Roman god with responsibility for the gates of heaven. Legend tells us he had two faces, one in the usual position and one on the back of his head, enabling him to see in both directions at once. From that Roman legend grew the idea that anybody able to see two sides to an argument, and agree with both, must have two faces just like Janus. This extends itself to meaning any person who is able to say one thing to one person and a conflicting thing to another must also need two faces, like Janus.

To **Set Off On The Wrong Foot** means to start something badly. This phrase finds us back with the Romans and their superstitions about left-sided things being evil and guided by evil spirits (the Latin word for left is 'sinister'). Gaius Petronius (AD 27–66), author of *Satyricon* and Emperor Nero's adviser in matters of luxury and extravagance, insisted his fellow Romans only ever entered or left a building by the right foot. Such was his obsession that guards were placed at the entrance to every public building to ensure his rule was obeyed. Most Romans shared Petronius's belief that to start a day by leaving the house by the left foot meant an unlucky day during which disaster might strike. (See also **Get Out Of Bed On The Wrong Side** and **Ears Are Burning**.)

Get Out Of Bed On The Wrong Side is a phrase we use when someone is being grumpy or bad tempered during the day. An ancient superstition suggests that evil spirits lay during the night on a particular side of the bed. It was unlucky to emerge in the morning on that side as it would mean those evil spirits and their influence would possess the body during its waking hours and this would only be put right the following dawn by not repeating the mistake. The wrong side, incidentally, is the left-hand side. (See also **Set Off On The Wrong Foot**.)

6: SPORT

Across The Board means all encompassing, wide-ranging and including everyone or everything. At 19th-century race meetings large boards would be used to display the odds on a horse to come first, second or third in a given race. A popular bet was to place an even amount of money on one horse to finish first, second or third. This was known as an 'across the board bet'. Obviously the bookmakers' odds would be calculated and only when a horse finished in the position a bookmaker least expected it to would a punter win more than the sum of his three stakes.

All Over Bar The Shouting is used when any controversial event is said to be technically settled, but arguments about the outcome continue, albeit with little effect on the result. In use since 1842, the phrase is from the world of sport, in particular boxing. Once a referee's decision was made, the crowds would either cheer or argue the judgement and shout appeals. But usually the referee's verdict stood and the contest would be over, apart from the subsequent cheering and shouting.

An **Also Ran** is memorable only for having no influence over events whatsoever and may as well have not been involved at all. This is an expression from the sport of horse racing, where the results are always listed in the order the bets may be paid – first, second and third. Others in the race would simply be listed under the heading, 'Also ran...'

When suggestions are **Bandied About** it means they are either put up for discussion or repeated by one party to many. For example, 'They bandied about the suggestion all afternoon before deciding not to proceed any further with it' or 'The lies she bandied about all over town did his reputation no good at all'. For the origin of the use of this word we travel to France and the game of Bander, which was an early form of tennis and involved hitting a ball to and fro. Later, in the 1600s, the Irish invented a team game that formed the origins of hockey, which required a group of people 'bandying' a ball between them. They called the sport 'Bander' after the French game because of the similarities between the two ideas. The crooked (or bowed) stick they used led to the term 'bandy-legged' being applied to those with bow legs.

When someone has **Lost Their Bottle** they have lost their nerve and their bravery. This phrase originates from the world of bare-knuckle prize-fighting during the late 19th and early 20th centuries. In a fighter's corner one of his seconds was known as 'the bottle man' and his job was to supply water to a fighter between rounds. Without water a fighter was unable to continue and sometimes it was known for a bottleman to be asked to walk away and leave when a fighter was taking a beating, to provide an excuse for him not continuing. The phrase 'lost his bottleman' was later shortened and widely used to describe cowardly behaviour.

Not enough room to **Swing A Cat** is a reference to small tight spaces. It is often thought the phrase originates from 17th-century sailors needing space in which they could swing the cat o' nine tails but there is other evidence from two centuries earlier. Cat lovers read no further. In the 15th century, there was a 'sport' involving the swinging of cats (by the tail) into the air where they would become moving targets for archers at fetes, fairs and country festivals. Crowded festivals would be described as having no room to 'swing the cat'.

To knock the **Daylights** out of somebody would be to put them on the receiving end of a pretty impressive beating. In days gone by 'daylights' was slang for a person's eyes. In early bare-knuckle boxing parlance, to darken a fighter's daylights would mean to give him a black eye, and to beat the daylights out of him meant both eyes were so badly swollen he could no longer see.

Down To The Wire is used to describe a contest, sporting or otherwise, where the outcome will not be determined until the very last. Before the days of televised horse racing, American and British racetracks would string a wire across the finishing line above the riders' heads. A steward would then be placed at a vantage point, looking down the line so that a winner could be more easily established during neck-and-neck finishes. In 1889 the following appeared in *Scribers Magazine*: 'As the end of the stand was reached, Timarch worked up to Petrel, and the two raced down to the wire, cheered on by the applause of the spectators. They ended the first half mile of the race head and head, passing lapped together under the wire, and beginning in earnest the mile which was yet to be traversed.' The race had gone 'down to the wire' and the expression has been widely used since then.

At The Drop Of A Hat is used to imply something would be carried out immediately. The phrase is easily traced to the 19th century when sporting referees, who usually wore hats, would raise one into the air, alerting competitors to be ready, and then drop it to signal the start of an event. The method was commonly used in boxing or horseracing and such events were considered started 'at the drop of a hat'. It is sometimes thought to be of American origin but the practice has long been used on both sides of the Atlantic.

A **Hat Trick** is the common phrase used to illustrate three of anything, but is most often associated with goals scored by footballers. But the origin of the phrase is found in a different sport, cricket. Traditionally any bowler dismissing three batsmen with three consecutive deliveries would be awarded a new cricket cap by his team in honour of the achievement, which became known as a 'hat trick'. Supporters at cricket matches seldom witness a hat trick as it only happens on rare occasions. In football it is far easier to achieve and thus much more common.

To **Keep It Up** means to persevere at a task and a person should carry on in the same manner. But what is 'it' – and why should it be 'up'? The origin for this can be found in the Victorian penchant for playing badminton in the gardens of country houses during summer months. Quite simply the shuttlecock needed to be kept up and the phrase 'keep it up' was frequently shouted during rallies.

To **Knuckle Down** means to concentrate and apply more effort to a task. Surprisingly this term emanates from the world of marbles where an important rule of the game is that the knuckle must be placed in the exact spot a player's previous marble had come to rest. Those not concentrating and playing carelessly with their knuckle off the ground would quite simply be told to put their 'knuckle down'.

To **Knuckle Under** means to submit and admit defeat. In the late 17th century when arguments raged in the drinking taverns of London, there was a custom that when a person admitted defeat he would knock the underside of a table with his knuckle. There is also a suggestion dating from around the same time that bare-knuckle prize-boxers would keep their fists down, with their knuckles under their hands, when they no longer wanted to fight, and to have them up facing an opponent when they did. Over the years this phrase has also corrupted to '**buckle under**'.

The **Mexican Wave** originated in 1981 at a University of Washington football match in America. According to the New York Times it came to the attention of the wider world during the World Cup in Mexico in 1986, which proved to be so boring that fans began to entertain themselves during dull matches. This provided a visual image copied by sports fans all over the world, often at cricket grounds where fans generally have a lot more time on their hands than at other sports.

When something gets done in the **Nick Of Time** it has been done at the very last possible minute, before it was too late. During the Middle Ages a tally man would keep the scores for team games. This chap would do so by carving a nick in a piece of wood each time a team scored and if the winning nick was added during the last minute it was known as the 'nick in time'.

To be **Out For A Duck** is a cricketing term meaning a batsman has been bowled out, or caught, without scoring any runs. The phrase was originally a 'duck's egg' and simply referred to the nought on the scoreboard which supposedly looked like the egg of a duck. It is probably another one of those old public schoolboy jokes.

To **Play Fast And Loose** is used to describe a person who cannot be trusted, usually with another's affections. Fast and loose was, for centuries, a popular gambling game played at race meetings, fairgrounds and market places all over Europe. Originally known as 'pin and girdle' it was played with loops made of leather straps being tossed over peg. The 'fast' in the phrase is used in the sense of an immovable object (the peg) and the 'loose' began as 'loops' before developing in the 15th century to become the idiom we have today. The game was apparently played with 'carefree abandon' which is how it became applied to the carefree and shallow attitude some of us adopt at times.

Taking Route One describes the fastest and most direct action to achieve a certain outcome. Usually this is the least elegant way to tackle something. It is a relatively modern expression that emerged during the 1980s and the sort of kick-and-run football that was played in England by the stars of the day. From almost anywhere on the pitch a player would simply lump the ball forward in the hope a teammate might make better use of it near the opponents' goalmouth. Fans soon tired of this sort of spectacle and commentators were labelling it 'Route One' football before the end of that decade. These days it can be used to explain any blunt and direct manner of dealing with problem solving.

To have somebody with a **Safe Pair Of Hands** deal with something for you is to have a person who is trustworthy, reliable and capable looking after your interests. This phase has its origins on the cricket fields of the British Empire during the 1800s, when anybody reliable in the field, especially when it came to catches, was said to have a safe pair of hands.

The phrase **To Come Up To Scratch** is closely linked. In early bare-knuckle boxing or prize-fighting bouts, long before the Marquis of Queensberry produced any rules, a line would be scratched in the ground midway between each fighter's corner at the start of the bout. Any boxer who was knocked down would be given 30 seconds to gather his senses and return to the scratch and show he was fit (or willing) enough to continue fighting. Any boxer 'coming up to the scratch' would be allowed to continue, but a boxer not coming up to the scratch was deemed the loser.

As Sick As A Parrot is another football cliché that has been used by the manager of a losing team. Liverpool footballer Phil Thompson is thought to have been the first to use it when he described his feelings after his team's defeat in the 1978 League Cup final. Some feel the phrase refers to the deadly viral disease among parrots that was transmitted to humans and killed many people in Africa in 1973, but others believe it has something to do with the famous Monty Python 'Dead Parrot' sketch of the 1960s. Finally, there is a school of thought that suggests parrots happily feed on rotting and fermenting (alcoholic) fruit – leading to the expression 'as pissed as a parrot' – after which they would be 'as sick as a parrot' the following day.

To **Start From Scratch** is a saying we use to illustrate starting again from the beginning, regardless of how much we have already achieved of a task. This is easily explained as during medieval horse races competitors would start at a line 'scratched' into the ground by either a sword or a javelin. If competitors cut corners, or strayed from the set course of the race, they would have to start again from the scratch.

To **Throw Your Hat Into The Ring** means you are signalling an intention to join an event or enterprise, or by taking up a challenge. The phrase can be traced back to the days of prize-fighters who would tour the country with travelling fairs giving local people the chance to win money by trying to beat them in the ring. The way any local would enter the competition was to throw his hat into the ring, which would then be placed in a pile with the others and later shown to the crowd as an invitation for the owner to step forward.

A **Turn Up For The Book** is a pleasant surprise, although not necessarily for everybody. This is a horse-racing phrase dating back to the time the sport was even shadier than it is now. A 'book' is traditionally a record of bets laid on a race kept by the bookmaker. There were occasions, when the favourites were backed heavily and expected to win, that a bookmaker could lose his livelihood on the outcome of a single race meeting. At these times it would be in his interest for an unfancied horse, with very few bets on it, to romp home in one of the last races and save the bookmaker's hide as he then got to keep all the money staked on more popular horses. The sport of kings had a relatively small community and it wasn't uncommon for favours to be called in at times. It was known that some owners would allow their champion horse to turn up and run under the name of an inferior nag, beat the field and thereby save a friendly bookmaker's business. As a result otherwise slow horses racing well and surprising 'everyone' by winning was known as a 'turn up for the book'. The horse had turned up especially to assist the bookmaker's book.

To have the **Upper Hand** implies a person will win a contest or social situation. This phrase dates back to the 15th century and a pastime involving two or more contestants. The first player grips a staff at the bottom end while the next places their hand just above it. This goes on, hand over hand, until the upper end of the shaft is reached: the last person to be able to take a grip has the 'upper hand'. This method of finding a random winner was often used in baseball and cricket in the 1900s when hands would be placed on a bat and the last to take a grip got to play the game first.

To be **Batting On A Sticky Wicket** is to be faced with a difficult problem that requires great care to resolve successfully. It is a cricketing term alluding to the difficulty a batsman has playing on a wet and tricky wicket. These days a wicket is protected from the rain by covers quickly pulled over if the clouds burst overhead. But earlier cricketers often played on a wet surface and great care was needed. The West Indian team fell foul of a 'sticky wicket' at the Kensington Oval in 1935 and it was later reported that the 'West Indians have a remarkable record here having only lost once in 1935 on a sticky pitch.'

A **Wild Goose Chase** is a fruitless pursuit with no hope of successful outcome. Its origin comes from the earliest form of horse racing during the 1500s in England. First the lead horse would be sent off in no particular direction with the rider able to choose his own route. After a delay a second rider would be sent off in pursuit, followed by all other competitors at regular intervals. As none of the pursuing riders knew which route the lead horse had taken they all set off in different directions akin to wild geese scurrying after their leader. The term was regularly applied to the sport but it appears to have been Shakespeare who altered the meaning to one of hopeless pursuit.

To **Win Hands Down** suggests a very comfortable victory. This is a widely used expression in the world of sport and its root can be found in the sport of kings, horse racing. Even today, when a jockey is winning comfortably he can gallop down the finishing straight without using his whip to encourage the nag along. Instead he can place both hands back on the reins, canter to the line and 'win with his hands down'.

To come **Within An Ace** of something is to get very close indeed. This is a dicing term, rather than a card expression as might seem obvious. In the game of dice the ace is the side with only one spot.

7: WORK AND TRADE

To go **Against The Grain** suggests something moving against the natural flow of events or feelings. For example, a wife, who hates football but will attend a Cup Final with her husband who loves the sport, might say, 'Well, even though it goes against the grain, I will go along.' It is a woodcutter's saying, in use since the 1600s. To work by cutting or carving along the grain of wood is notably easier than cutting across (or against) the grain. Working with the grain is considered smooth and easy; against it is hard and unnatural.

At Full Blast is associated with something going at full speed or operating at the maximum limit. Back during the Industrial Revolution foundries would use a huge blast furnace for the smelting of iron. When the foundry was at the limit of its production it would be regarded as 'operating at full blast'.

If we are not fit to **Hold A Candle** to somebody it means we are not in their league and should not be working in the same place. This phrase is traceable to the day when craftsmen would employ unskilled labour (usually children) to hold candles illuminating their work. Being told one wasn't fit to 'hold the candle' was an insult indeed and usually used as a derogatory term to an inferior craftsman or street entertainer.

To **Carry The Can** means to take reluctant responsibility for something, usually that has gone wrong. Originally a military term, the saying stems from the duty of one man to carry a large can (bucket) of beer between the mess and a group of men. The one carrying the can was responsible for both the beer and for returning the empty bucket. The phrase was in regular use by 1936 but a second theory dates further back. During the 19th century, explosive was regularly used in both coal and tin mines. One person would be given the unenviable task of carrying a can of explosives to the mine face each day, hence a reluctance to 'carry the can'.

When the **Cat Is Let Out Of The Bag** it means some sort of secret has been revealed. In the days of the medieval market deceptions were often played on unsuspecting buyers, and one of those involved piglets and cats. Having been shown a suckling piglet a purchaser would then start haggling with the vendor over price. While this was going on the piglet would be bagged up ready to be taken home but a cat was often substituted while the buyer's attention was diverted. The deception would only be revealed when the buyer reached home and let a 'cat out of the bag'.

If we are told we have **Our Work Cut Out For Us** we know there is a lot to be done and a difficult task lies ahead. The phrase stems from the craft of tailoring but at first glance it would seem the work is being made easier (by having someone cut out patterns before the stitching begins). But, in fact, such a practice makes life more difficult for the tailor, as cutting the work out in advance is much quicker than actually tailoring a suit and therefore piles of material would mount up making it hard for the tailor to keep up. Therefore it is quite easy to imagine a tailor explaining he is busy as he has his 'work cut out for him' and would be hard at it for the foreseeable future. The first recorded appearance of the phrase meaning 'more than one can handle' turned up in *A Christmas Carol*, a Charles Dickens novel first published in 1843.

Don't Let The Bastards Grind You Down is a modern saying, usually used by way of encouragement to a person under pressure. The origin of the expression possibly comes from a 17th-century carpentry tool called a bastard file – a coarse file that was designed to smoothe out rough abrasions prior to using a finishing file. Using a bastard file is a heavy-handed way to grind something down.

In 1993 the Conservative MP Michael Mates resigned as Minister for Northern Ireland after it was revealed he had sent the fugitive businessman Asil Nadir a watch with the inscription 'Don't Let the Bastards Grind You Down.' Presumably by that he meant his own colleagues, as the government of the day was seeking to have Nadir extradited and brought to justice in Britain. Nadir had once paid Mates to ask questions on his behalf in the House of Commons in the famous 'cash for questions' scandal of the early 1990s. In 1993 Nadir fled Britain as he was about to stand trial for fraud and has never returned. So serious was the situation that Peter Diamond, the pilot who flew Nadir to Turkey on a private jet, received a two-year jail sentence for committing an act intended to pervert the course of justice. The bastards never did grind Nadir down, nor, indeed, catch up with him.

The expression **Dyed In The Wool** is used to describe somebody who is fixed in their opinions and inflexible. The phrase came into use in English wool mills and is first recorded in 1579. Quite simply wool that had been dyed before it was treated would retain its colour much better than if it were dyed after weaving (known as 'dyed in the piece'). Therefore 'dyed in the wool' became a phrase applied to anything that wasn't easily altered by other processes, such as persuasion.

Fired – Prior to the invention of toolboxes all English craftsmen and tradesmen carried their tools around in a sack. To be given their sack meant being discharged from employment and the worker would carry his tools either home or on to his next job (see

The Sack). However, miners who were caught stealing coal or other materials, such as copper or tin, would have their tools confiscated and burned at the pit head in front of the other shift workers, a punishment that became known as 'firing the tools' or 'being fired'. This meant the offender would be unable to find other work and repeat his crime elsewhere. Other trades adopted the practice and the phrase quickly established itself.

Mad As A Hatter is a term used to describe unpredictable behaviour. In the Middle Ages making felt hats involved the use of a highly toxic substance called mercurous nitrate. This acid was known to cause trembling in some people, a little like the symptoms of Parkinson's Disease, and those who suffered the effects in this way were assumed to be mad or crazy. During the 17th century tales were told of a man called Robert Crab, an eccentric who lived in Chesham, who was easily identified because of his distinctive hat and was known to locals as 'the mad hatter'. He apparently gave away all his wealth to the poor and lived his life eating anything he could find in the countryside, such as grass, berries and dock leaves. The phrase passed over into the English language in the 19th century, thanks to

Lewis Carroll and his novel *Alice In Wonderland*. In the story Carroll invented a mad hatter but he may have been inspired by a real-life figure.

To **Strike While The Iron Is Hot** means to take action early enough, ensuring a favourable result. The phrase is a medieval blacksmith's term, alluding to shaping an iron horseshoe at exactly the time the metal was at the correct temperature and not giving it time to cool, when it would become harder to work with.

Having **Too Many Irons In The Fire** is an extension of the expression, originating at around the same time. It means that a person has too many activities taking place at one time, preventing them from giving enough time to any one of them. It must be tempting for a blacksmith to try and speed up his work by having more irons in his fire than he is capable of working with. The result would be that all of them either became too hot and soft, or cooled down again before he has had time to shape some of them properly.

If somebody is described as **On The Level** it means they are trustworthy and reliable. In the 14th century the freemasons' membership was exclusively made up of skilled stone workers. A level base or platform for a building or other structure was the most important part of a whole building project. Because of that the 'level' used to ensure a flat foundation was the most important tool a freemason had in his case, leading to a common phrase at the time describing anything, including a person, as 'level' (true, honest and dependable).

A **Nation Of Shopkeepers** is an insult to the English usually attributed to Napoleon Bonaparte, who once said, on being told the English were preparing for war, *'L'Angleterre est une nation de boutiquiers.'* But once the fighting was over, and Napoleon's professional, heavily armed and well-trained army had been trounced at Waterloo by the shelf-stackers, it was discovered that the expression was not original. In 1776 Adam Smith wrote in his book *An Inquiry into the Nature and Causes of the Wealth of Nations*: 'To found a great empire for the sole purpose of raising up a people of customers may, at first sight, appear a project fit only for a nation of shopkeepers. It is, however, a project altogether unfit for a nation of shopkeepers, but extremely fit for a nation whose government is influenced by shopkeepers.'

The same year Josiah Tucker, the Dean of Gloucester, an economist and writer, used a similar expression in his essay entitled *A Series of Answers to Certain Popular Objections Against Separating from the Rebellious Colonies*: 'And what is true of a shopkeeper is true of a shop keeping nation.' He was writing about the American War of Independence.

Something going at **Nineteen To The Dozen** is operating very quickly indeed. Back in the 18th century coal-fired, steam-driven pumps were used to clear water out of Cornish tin and copper mines. Hand-powered pumps were slow and ineffective but at full power the steam version could clear 19,000 gallons of water for every dozen bushels of coal burned, which is how the expression became used.

An **Operating Theatre** is an unusual name for such a place. Why not operating room, suite or ward? The answer can be found with the first operating suite, built in London in 1822. The Old Operating Theatre in London was built on the original site of St Thomas's Hospital and is still complete today and open as a medical museum.

Purpose-built, the Old Operating Theatre was designed as an amphitheatre, with rows of seating enabling trainee surgeons and young doctors to observe operations. Subsequent rooms for this purpose were originally known as Anatomical Theatres, because many surgeons would lecture students while carrying out operations and these events often became something of a performance. One leading surgeon of the day, Sir Astley Paston Cooper (1768–1841), became famous for his theatrical performances. In 1789 Cooper was appointed demonstrator of anatomy at St Thomas's Hospital and could command as much as the equivilant of £23,000 in today's money for a single theatrical perfomance.

When something is described as **Out Of Sorts** we can expect it to be jumbled and disorganised. If a person is described in such a way we would realise they are not in great health, low in spirit and generally in poor form. This is an old printing expression dating back to the time when presses used cast or carved letters organised into rows to print on to paper. These letters were known as 'sorts'. If a printer was short of the letters he needed, some might be either replaced by others that were similar or perhaps left out altogether. Such a jumble would reveal to the reader that the printer was 'out of sorts'.

To **Pay On The Nail** means to make a prompt cash payment for good or services. Back in the bustling medieval market place, dealers were known by their round, pillar-like counters, called nails. It is thought the phrase referred to the practice of a buyer placing his cash openly and in full public view on the nail. This routine is recognised to this day by the four bronze nails that still stand outside the Exchanges in Bristol and Limerick. The expression is not unique to Britain, however: Holland and Germany have a similar saying.

To make a **Pig's Ear** out of something is to attempt a task and get it so badly wrong the effort is useless. The phrase dates back to the Middle Ages when it is said that the only part of a pig that could not be eaten or used in any way was the ear. Therefore, any craftsman or (usually) apprentice making something ineffective or unusable was considered to have produced a 'pig's ear'.

A **Ploughman's Lunch** is a meal of fresh bread, cheese, pickles and onion. It can be found on the menu of just about every British pub, even those without a ploughed field in sight. It is usually thought to be the traditional packed lunch of a ploughman – a romantic reminder of simple life in the English countryside during its golden years. In fact the phrase has nothing at all to do with the traditional working ploughman. It was invented in the early 1970s by the English Country Cheese Council as part of a successful marketing campaign, and first used in an article written by its chairman. Now that is clever marketing.

To **Stretch A Point** is to exceed or to suggest something beyond what is usually acceptable. The phrase alludes to the tagged laces in 18th-century costume which were called 'points'. To 'truss a point' meant to tie the laces together and to 'stretch a point' meant to allow them to adjust and provide room for growth beyond the clothing's original intended size, such as after a feast or during early pregnancy.

A **Pot Boiler** is a derisory term for a piece of work by an artist or writer. It is sometimes misused in the case of domestic soap operas to suggest the drama is so good that the 'pot is kept boiling' for another week. But this expression for creative folk completing work well below their abilities stems from working simply to earn money. Such work was supposed to ensure a steady flow of income for a family and kept food bubbling in the kitchen pot, until a more suitable commission was offered.

To find yourself in **Queer Street** is to be in some sort of financial trouble, possibly even bankrupt. The phrase originates from the word 'query' which tradesmen and merchants would write in their ledgers against the column of customers who were late in paying. The word would be written as a reminder to enquire of the debt the next time that person attended their premises for business. Carey Street, off Chancery Lane in London, housed the bankruptcy courts and through that became affectionately known as 'Queer Street'.

When somebody **Queers Your Pitch** they are deliberately attempting to prevent a successful outcome to your venture. During the 18th and 19th centuries market traders began calling the area set aside for their barrows and stalls a 'pitch', a term still used in Britain's market places. It is not clear why the word 'pitch' was adopted as market slang but it could possibly have links to 'pitching' an idea. For hundreds of years prior to that the word 'queer' had been used as English slang for anything that was wrong or worthless. In the vibrant and competitive market places of centuries gone by it was common practice for rival traders to attempt to spoil each other's trade, sometimes in an underhand way and sometimes legitimately by using better banter or cheaper goods. Rendering a rival stall worthless became known as 'queering a pitch'.

Later in the century stage actors adopted the phrase when other cast members stole the audience's attention during a scene, evidence of which can be found in an 1866 review of Shakespeare's *Macbeth*. 'The smoke and fumes of "blue fire" which had been used to illuminate the fight came up through the chinks of the stage, fit to choke a dozen Macbeths, and – pardon the little bit of professional slang – poor Jamie's "pitch" was "queered" with a vengeance.'

When something is **Run Of The Mill** it is ordinary and uninspiring. In the great mill towns of England cotton and wool used to be mass-produced and exported the world over. Great fortunes were made on the quality of material a mill produced and quality control checks were an important part of business. After each mill run some material would be found to be inferior to the rest and this was set aside as 'run of the mill' cotton to be trimmed and used in other ways.

When something has **Run Out Of Steam** it has run out of energy and motion. All enthusiasm has been lost. This is an expression dating from the Industrial Revolution and the invention of giant steam engines that were used to power machinery, trains and ships. Entire factories relied upon steam power and when the steam ran out, everything connected to the engine ground to a halt.

To be **Given The Sack** is to lose your job, or be discharged from duty. This expression dates back to the day when craftsmen, tradesmen and labourers would travel from place to place, sometimes working on a project for only a few days and at other times for many years. Long before toolboxes, these workers would carry the tools of their trade around in a large sack, which would be given to their employer for safe keeping and then returned when their services were no longer needed. To be given the sack was to be given the means to carry their tools to another place of work, unlike being **Fired** when the tradesman had been caught stealing or breaking the rules, and his tools would be burned to ensure he would be unable to work elsewhere.

Shit is an ugly word but it does have an interesting origin. Dried manure and barnyard dung have long been used by the farming industry as a soil fertiliser and were often transported around the British Isles in boats and ships. But it soon became obvious that the lower holds were a dangerous place to store them because when manure becomes damp it begins to give off methane gas. Sometimes this led to explosions, after a build-up of methane gases in the holds, and several ships sank as a consequence. Once the reason for the explosions was discovered, it became common practice for this type of cargo to be stored in the drier upper decks and for it to have the words 'Store High In Transit' or 'Ship High In Transit' stamped on the containers. Before long dockers were unloading crates full of manure with the letters 'S.H.I.T.' stamped along the sides.

Being **Tarred With The Same Brush** is to be part of a group regarded as all having the same faults and weaknesses but, by inference, often unfairly. The expression is an old farming term, which derives from the practice of treating the sores of an entire flock of sheep. The sores could be coated by a brush dipped in tar. The same brush would be used on all of the stricken sheep but never on a healthy animal for fear of passing the infection on, in which case all infected sheep were 'tarred with the same brush'.

If a person is **Never Going To Set The Thames Alight** they are unlikely ever to do anything impressive or notable, usually in respect of either their work or studies. Many believe the allusion here is to the river Thames but the root of our expression is actually a 'temse'. During the 1700s farmers used a tool called a temse, which was a sieve given to labourers or farmhands during the harvest months. Hard-grafting farm boys would joke with each other they had worked so fast their temse had caught fire. Equally, lazy scallywags would 'never be able to set their temse alight'.

Being **On Tenterhooks** means being under great stress or tension while waiting for a result or outcome. It has been suggested the phrase stems from tent hooks, which are used to hold a canvas under great tension, keeping it watertight, but its origin is far older. In bygone days newly produced cloth would be attached to hooks and stretched across large frames known as 'tenters', coming from the Latin word 'tendere', meaning 'to stretch out'. Anyone, or anything, stretched to the limit later became known as being 'on tenterhooks'.

8: THE BIBLE

The **Apple Of One's Eye** is somebody (usually a child) who is regarded as precious and irreplaceable. Over a thousand years ago, the pupil of the eye was known as the 'apple'. The modern word, pupil, is Latin and did not form part of the English language until the 1500s. Sight was regarded as the most valued of all the senses and therefore the 'apple' was precious and irreplaceable. King Alfred, in the late ninth century, actually linked the two and applied it to somebody he was affectionate towards, but it is not known who. The first recorded reference is in the Bible: Deuteronomy 32:10 says, 'He kept him as the apple of his eye,' suggesting he watched over him to ensure his safety.

The **Blind Leading The Blind** is a phrase used to suggest the incompetent and stupid are advising others, equally incapable, in matters they know nothing about. In short, none of them has a clue. This is a simple expression found in the Bible, where the line 'Let them alone: they be blind leaders of the blind. And if the blind lead the blind, both shall fall into the ditch' appears in Mathew 15:14. This is the generally accepted origin, but the sacred Hindu treatises *Katha Upanishad* contain a quotation thought to be in the region of 3,000 years old. The ancient text includes the line: 'Abiding in the midst of ignorance and believing themselves wise and learned, fools go aimlessly hither and thither, like the blind led by the blind.'

Other variations could be equally fitting, such as the bland leading the bland, or even the blonde leading the blonde.

At The Eleventh Hour indicates something has occurred at the very last moment. First used in the Bible (Matthew 20:9), the phrase can be traced to the parable of the labourers and the practice of a 12-hour working day. In the vineyards the very last of the day's labourers would be taken on during the eleventh hour (around 5pm) in an effort to finish the day's scheduled work on time.

To have **Feet Of Clay** suggests a real weakness in something (or someone) otherwise considered strong and infallible. This is a Biblical phrase and comes from a story in the Book of Daniel 2:31–5. Daniel describes a 'great statue' in Nebuchadnezzar's dream, which had a head of gold, breast and arms of silver, stomach and thighs of brass, legs of iron and feet of iron mixed with clay. But iron doesn't mix easily with clay, leaving a great weakness in an otherwise mighty monument that is not obvious to the eye.

Having a **Fly In The Ointment** is an expression used to describe a tiny thing that is hindering the outcome of something altogether much larger and more important. Thousands of years ago, before doctors, apothecaries (an early version of chemists) dealt with all medical treatment, and their sought-after potions and ointments would be dispensed from large vats. These vats could treat a vast number of people but a single fly or other insect found floating in them was thought to spoil the whole amount. The earliest reference to this phrase can be found in the Bible, in Ecclesiastes (10:1), which includes the phrase 'Dead flies cause the ointment of the apothecary to send forth a stinking savour.'

Somebody **Playing The Fool** is usually an irritating character, although not necessarily in a harmful way. This is a biblical expression with its origin in the book of Samuel 26:21. The story tells of King Saul, who admits to following David and trying to have him killed. 'I have sinned, return, my son David. I will no more do you harm because my soul is precious in thine eyes this day. Behold, I have played the fool and have erred exceedingly.' Although in Saul's case playing the fool had had a sinister intention, in modern times it is not regarded with anything like the seriousness of trying to have somebody killed.

The **Powers That Be** seem to get everywhere. They are the unseen authority making plans and rules for us all. This is another biblical idiom: Romans 13:1 reads, 'Let every soul be subject unto the higher powers. For there is no power but of God: the powers that be are ordained of God.'

The **Road To Damascus** is an expression used to describe an epiphany or any other life-changing experience. This is a popular biblical expression, referring to the day that Saul was travelling along the road to Damascus on his way to persecute the Christians there. Acts 9: 3–5 says, 'And as he journeyed, he came near Damascus and suddenly there shined a light around him from heaven. And he fell to earth and heard a voice saying unto him, "Saul, Saul. Why do thou persecute me?" And he replied, "Who art thou, Lord?" And the Lord said, "I am Jesus whom thou persecute, it is hard for thee to kick against the pricks."

Then Saul was suddenly struck blind and it apparently took him three days to recover. When he did, he changed his name to Paul and converted to Christianity. This story is also the root of the well-known expression **To See The Light**, used to describe a person who has eventually seen the error of their ways and corrected them.

To be made a **Scapegoat** is to take responsibility for, and be blamed for, another's mistakes. This phrase dates back to an ancient Hebrew ritual for the Day Of Atonement set out by Moses himself in his *Laws Of Moses*. He decided that two goats should be taken to the altar of the tabernacle where the high priest would draw lots for the Lord and for Azazel (a desert demon). The goat selected as the Lord's would then be sacrificed and, by confession, the high priest would transfer all of his, and his people's, sins on to the second goat. The lucky mammal would then be sent into the wilderness, taking all the sins with it. If only it were that easy these days.

The **Final Straw** is a small insignificant event producing a situation that is intolerable overall. It has a Biblical origin and an old proverb states, 'It is the last straw that breaks the laden camel's back', which means that one small thing may bring about a catastrophe in the greater scheme of events. In the 17th and 18th centuries the expression in England used to be 'the last feather that breaks the horse's back' but Charles Dickens rescued the old proverb in his novel *Dombey And Son* in 1848. It caught on so successfully that it is 'last straws' and not 'last feathers' we talk about today.

A **Stumbling Block** is an obstacle, either physical or emotional, which holds up progress or causes some other difficulty. The Bible is the source of this popular phrase, as the Book of Romans 14:13 states: 'Let us therefore not judge one another any more: but judge this rather, that no man put a stumbling block or any occasion to fall in his brother's way.'

To **Separate The Wheat From The Chaff** means to divide the valuable from the worthless. It is easy to see how, during a harvest, it is important to thresh corn to separate the grain from the husk. But the answer to how it became a popular and widely used expression can be found in the Bible and the suggestion that the 'wheat' are those loyal to Christ, and the 'chaff' are those who have rejected his ideals. Luke 3:17 has a passage including the line 'His winnowing fork is in his hand to clear his threshing floor and to gather the wheat into his barn, but he will burn up the chaff in his fire.'

A **Wolf In Sheep's Clothing** is a person who appears pleasant and friendly but carries a hidden menace. This expression can be found in another of Aesop's fables, dating back 1,400 years. In one of his stories a wolf wraps himself up in a sheep's fleece and sneaks past the shepherd into the paddock. Once inside he immediately eats one of the lambs before his deception can be discovered. But the actual origin can be found in the Bible: Matthew 7:15 says, 'Beware of false prophets, which come to you in sheep's clothing. Inwardly they are ravening wolves.'

9: PEOPLE AND PLACES

To be doing something **All On Your Tod** means you are completely alone with no help or assistance from anybody else. This is partly cockney rhyming slang and partly the story of a man who began his life on his own and ended it in the same way.

James Forman 'Tod' Sloan was born on 10 August 1874 in Indiana, the son of a Union soldier. His mother died when he was only five years old and his father soon sent him to live with a nearby family where he was largely left to his own devices. A solitary child, he found work at the nearby oil fields but soon found himself with a job at a horse-racing stable in St. Louis, where he lived in the stables. By the time he was 11 years old he had moved to Kansas City after being employed by a racehorse trainer as a stable lad. At only 12 years old he was working at the Latonia race track in Kentucky when he was given an opportunity to ride a racehorse and, despite finishing last, he was immediately hooked on horse racing.

Within ten years Sloan was dominating the racing scene on the east coast of America by using his famous 'monkey man' crouching style, since used by most professional jockeys. Sloan was so good that within a few years he was winning an incredible 46 per cent of all the races he entered. He was soon brought to England and in 1901 he was installed as the Prince of Wales' senior jockey. By this time the loner from Indiana was surrounded by the rich and famous, the great and the good, travelling everywhere with his own personal valet.

But the good life was not to last. Despite his spectacular success, the hierarchy of the British Jockey Club hated the American and his larger than life personality and before the end of the season officials had persuaded the Prince not to renew his racing contract. With that, his licence was revoked for unspecified reasons, although the rumour was that Sloan had been illegally betting on races in which he was competing. He was then all but ostracized by the racing communities in both England and America. Although he managed to use some of his wealth to convert a small bistro in Paris into the famous Harry's New York Bar, financial problems forced him back to America, where he lived out his remaining days alone and in debt, dying of cirrhosis of the liver in 1933.

But his fame was secured and the mark he made on the racing scene has never really diminished. George M. Cohen's endearing song *Yankee Doodle Dandy* was based on Sloan's sad life and in England Londoners awarded the jockey with their highest accolade: a piece of cockney rhyming slang. For ever more the expression to be 'all on your tod' means 'all alone like Tod Sloan'. Even his autobiography was called, *Tod Sloan – by Himself.*

The **Blurb** is the curious name given to a short, written promotional sales pitch. Loosely speaking it is a rough but positive general explanation. The American comedy writer Gelet Burgess invented a comic book in 1907, which featured a Miss Belinda Blurb on the cover. The publication was to be given away at a book festival and Belinda was a parody of the type of artwork often found on the jackets of more serious novels at the time. When later asked what the name meant, Burgess described it as 'self praise and making a noise like a publisher'. A simple example of inspired alliteration, the phrase caught on immediately.

As Bold As Brass is applied to anyone with the courage of their conviction and not afraid to be seen either succeeding or failing. It is recorded that the phrase dates back to the late 1770s and refers to a London magistrate called Brass Crosby. At that time it was illegal for the workings of Parliament to be published for public knowledge. However, one London printer produced a pamphlet revealing some of the proceedings and was immediately arrested. He was brought before Brass Crosby's court and the magistrate, in tune with public opinion, let the printer off. Crosby was immediately arrested for treason and himself thrown in jail. But such was the public outcry in support of the magistrate that Brass was released and he became something of a hero. His brave stand against authority was widely reported, leading to the term 'as bold as brass' passing into common parlance.

To **Stage A Boycott** means withdrawing from social or commercial arrangements, either as a protest or punishment. The phrase is one of remarkably few to emanate from southern Ireland. In the 1870s Captain Charles Cunningham Boycott, an Englishman, was working as a land agent for Lord Earne at Loughmask in County Mayo. In September 1880 a campaign, organised by the Irish Land League, was calling for a reform of the system of landholding, and protesting tenants demanded Captain Boycott initiate a substantial reduction in their rents. Boycott refused, even ordering anyone in arrears be evicted, whereupon Charles Parnell, the President of the Land League, made a speech calling for everybody in the local community, not only Boycott's tenants, to refuse to have anything to do with the unpopular agent.

The result was that labourers refused to work for him, shop and innkeepers declined to serve either him or his family and even the postal staff refused to deliver his letters. Boycott had to go to the expense of having his food brought in, under guard, from great distances away, and of employing 50 labourers from as far away as Ulster for the harvest, all protected by 900 guard. This action by the locals was so successful and aroused so much passion (it was even reported in *The Times* during November 1880) that the Land League called upon all Irish men and women to treat similar landlords, or their agents, like 'Boycott'. Within weeks the phrase was adopted by newspapers around Europe and subsequently worldwide. By the time the captain died in 1887, after returning to England, his name had become a standard part of the English language.

A **Cock And Bull** story is likely to be untrue and without any real facts supporting it. Some suggest the phrase originates from old fables in which animals speak to each other, but there is a much more reliable source. Stony Stratford is a Buckinghamshire town located almost directly halfway between London and Birmingham and Oxford and Cambridge respectively. During the great coaching era of the late 18th and early 19th centuries, the town was an important and thriving stop-over point for travellers, tradesmen and mail coaches. The two main coaching inns were called The Cock and The Bull and both became known throughout the country as the centre of all news travelling either on foot or by horse. The competing inns established a rivalry as to which could produce the most exciting and scurrilous travellers' tales to be passed on to the major cities and as a result many unbelievable stories were dismissed as 'Cock and Bull' tales.

Codswallop means that something is worthless, rubbish or nonsense. Wallop is Australian slang for beer or ale. In 1875 Australian inventor Hiram Codd developed the first bottle with a lid which kept sparkling water fizzy until it was opened, but Aussie beer drinkers were unimpressed by the new craze of drinking fizzy water, which they regarded as rubbish, and dismissed it as 'Codd's Wallop'.

If something is **Too Dicey** it is considered to be risky or dubious and should be treated with great caution. The BBC's *Antiques Roadshow* suggested an origin for this phrase in May 1999 when a presenter was given an antique map to value. He explained to the owner that there was once a crooked map-seller who, in the 1800s, used old and worn map plates to print new copies on to old paper and sell them on as original antiques. The map seller was called Mr Dicey and when he was

157

caught and punished the phrase entered the language as a byword for anything that could not be relied upon.

We are often told that everybody will have their **Fifteen Minutes Of Fame** at some point in their lives. It is a world famous expression usually applied to those who deliberately make public fools out of themselves to become well known to a wider audience. Most people attribute the expression to the American artist and filmmaker Andy Warhol (1928–1987) and it can be traced to his first International Retrospective Exhibition at the Moderna Museum in Stockholm, Sweden in 1968. The exhibition catalogue carried the line: 'In the future everybody will be world famous for fifteen minutes.' It soon became the most famous of all Warhol's quotes, despite the fact it may have been written by a magazine copy editor. To this day it is the only quote of Warhol's that most people know.

Warhol was perhaps quite prophetic in his observation, predicting a society where the talentless and superficial would earn the sort of recognition that those who spend many years learning an instrument, sport or other worthwhile function in life sometimes fail to achieve. In 1969 Warhol would probably have had no idea how this might manifest itself in the future, because in those days children didn't grow up with the ambition to become famous in the world by being photographed in their pants for a magazine or newspaper and young girls didn't tell their careers master they wanted to grow up to become a footballer's girlfriend, or wife, or both.

But in 1979 Warhol possibly saw the future when he commented, 'It's the place where my prediction from the 1960s finally came true: "In the future everyone will be famous for fifteen minutes." But I'm bored with that line. I never use it any more. My new line is, "In fifteen minutes everybody will be famous."'

The **Full Monty** means the whole lot – the maximum available. There are several suggestions for its origin but the earliest can be traced back to the turn of the century. In 1904 the tailors Montague Burton (later shortened to Burtons) established their first hire shop in Chesterfield. They made it possible for men not only to hire a suit for special occasions, but also to hire a complete outfit of suit, shirt, tie, shoes and socks and those opting for the full set were known to be wearing the 'Full Monty'. The saying re-emerged in the mid-1980s as part of the *Coronation Street* dictionary *Street Talk*. It has since been used as the title of several books and a film.

To have **Hobson's Choice** is to have no choice at all. In the early 1600s Thomas Hobson owned a well-known livery stable in Cambridge. Hobson insisted on hiring out his horses strictly on a rotation basis to ensure each animal was evenly worked and nobody was allowed to select a favourite, as was common practice in other liveries at the time. The author and poet John Milton seems to be responsible for the phrase passing into wider English use as he mentions Hobson in two of his epitaphs. Milton was at Cambridge University around 1630 so it is quite possible he was one of Hobson's customers.

Less Is More is an expression usually used to illustrate that simplicity is always better than a complicated option. It is a proverb that emerged during the 1900s and was originally attributed to the German furniture designer Ludwig Mies Van Der Rohe (1886–1969), who is widely regarded as one of the pioneers of modern architecture. He created the influential 20th-century architecture based upon extreme simplicity. His buildings are made with modern materials such as steel and plate glass that he called 'skin and bones designing'. His buildings stand as a monument to his 'Less is More' design techniques in major cities throughout the world.

The Real McCoy is the genuine article, not a fake or a copy. One story goes back to the 1890s. American welterweight boxer Kid McCoy dominated his sport during the late 19th century and was well known throughout his land. McCoy had many imitators who would earn money in boxing booths and fairgrounds all across America, challenging locals to take on the champion. In the end few people believed, and rightly so, the champion was fighting in booths. During the 1920s, long after McCoy had retired, the little boxer was having a quiet drink in a bar when a lumbering drunk picked an argument with him. McCoy's associates warned the giant off by insisting he was provoking a champion boxer but the fat man would have none of it, challenging McCoy to prove who he was. Eventually the ageing boxer reluctantly floored the persistent drinker with a single punch and then went back to his whisky. Apparently when the man regained consciousness his first words were 'Godammit, he *is* the real McCoy.' It's a great story, but it isn't the origin of the expression.

Elijah McCoy was born in Colchester, Ontario, Canada, on 2 May 1844, the son of former slaves who had fled north from Kentucky. McCoy trained as a mechanical engineer in Scotland before travelling to America and settling in Detroit. In 1872 he designed an automatic lubricator for steam engines, his first of 57 patented inventions to revolutionise industry in America. Others included the ironing board and the lawn sprinkler. McCoy became famous and his popular inventions were copied all over the world, although many buyers would insist on buying only 'the real McCoy'.

A **Mickey Finn** is a drink that has been drugged in one way or another, usually to render a person helpless so that a crime can be committed. Mickey Finn was the owner of both the Palm Garden Restaurant and the Lone Star Saloon located on Whiskey Row, Chicago. Neither establishment was quite what it seemed; both were havens for pickpockets and petty thieves, mostly trained by Finn himself. One of Finn's common methods was to lace drinks with chloral hydrate (knock-out drops) and then fleece his victims before dumping them down the road. Unsurprisingly the two bars were closed down in 1903, although Finn escaped jail and found work as a barman where he sold his recipe to other unscrupulous vagabonds.

A **Monkey Wrench** is an adjustable spanner or wrench which is versatile and in use all over the world. Almost every builder and engineer owns a monkey wrench. But why is it called 'monkey'? The answer is simply that the popular tool was invented, and made – during the 1700s in England – by a London blacksmith called Charles Moncke.

His Name Is Mud is a derogatory phrase used to describe a person who is unpopular or completely out of favour due to some act. The obvious allusion might seem to be one of someone so low in society's opinion that they are no better than mud, but this is not the origin of the phrase. On 14 April 1865 John Wilkes Booth assassinated President Abraham Lincoln in the Ford Theater, Washington DC. As he

163

made his escape Booth broke his leg, but still managed to reach his horse and ride away. When he reached the countryside he looked for the house of Dr Samuel Mudd who treated his injury. Mudd had no idea of the events of the evening but, when he heard of the assassination the following day, he immediately informed the authorities he had seen Booth. Despite his innocence, the doctor was arrested and later convicted of conspiracy and sentenced to life imprisonment. In 1869 Mudd was pardoned and released from jail, but the American public never forgave him for his implied involvement in the assassination plot. It would be another hundred years before Mudd was finally declared innocent and his name cleared.

Murphy's Law is the theory that if anything can go wrong it probably will. This phrase began to be used in 1949 at the Edwards Air Force Base test centre in California. Captain Edward A Murphy was an engineer working on Project MX981, which was a series of experiments to find out how much deceleration the human body can stand in a plane crash. One morning Murphy found a transducer had been wired up the wrong way and wasn't working. The young engineer fixed the problem and claimed of the technician responsible 'If there is ever a wrong way to do something, he will find it.' During the tests the project manager kept a list of theories, or 'laws' as he called them, and added Murphy's comment under the title 'Murphy's Law'. A little later Dr John Paul Stapp, an Air Force doctor, was involved in similar deceleration experiments and gave a press conference to reveal his team's results. During the press session Dr Stapp recorded that the project's excellent safety record was due to a firm belief in 'Murphy's Law', which was to try and foresee anything that could go wrong and avoid it happening by advanced planning. Over the following years aerospace manufacturers picked upon the phrase and used it widely in their advertising, leading to 'Murphy's Law' becoming used all over the English-speaking world.

When we describe something as **OK**, we regard it as acceptable and good for use. The expression seems to have first appeared in print during 1839 in the *Boston Morning Post* and later popularised during the 1840 election campaign of Martin Van Buren of Kinderhook, New York. He was known as 'Old Kinderhook' – OK for short. Twenty years later, during the American Civil War, soldiers relied on a biscuit called Orrin Kendall for rations, and a port in Haiti called Aux Cayes was famous among American sailors for its rum, known as 'OK Rum'. But before all of this there lived a popular native American chief called Old Keokuk who signed all his treaties by using only his initials.

A **Parting Shot** is a final blow or withering remark that a victim has no chance of responding to. The Parthians were an ancient race living in south-west Asia. They were skilled warriors whose battle tactics included mounted archers riding away from their enemy, giving the impression of a retreat. They would then twist backwards in their saddles and fire with deadly accuracy at the pursuing enemy. The first references were made to the Parthians in English literature during the 17th century and the phrase 'parthian shot' became a well-known phrase for 'parting blow' until the early 20th century when the similarity between 'parthian' and 'parting' led to a corruption of the original phrase.

A **Peeping Tom** is a male person who tries to watch something they shouldn't – usually with sexual connotations – in the hope nobody catches them. The expression has a wonderful origin connected to everybody's favourite naked horsewoman, Lady Godiva. During the 11th century the Earl of Mercia, Leofric, was one of the three great English earls and he ruled a vast area of the country. In 1040, according to legend, he tried to impose heavy taxes on his countrymen and there was uproar in the streets. Leofric's compassionate and charitable wife Godgifu (which has evolved into Godiva) sided with the people and begged her husband to lower the taxes. Leofric told his wife he would lower taxes after she had ridden naked through the streets of Coventry. Now Godiva was a game girl and her hapless husband hadn't reckoned on her spirit, so she agreed to the challenge. Not surprisingly the people of Coventry were delighted but as a show of respect all agreed to stay indoors, close their shutters and face the other way as the lady passed by. All of them kept their word, except Tom the Tailor who couldn't help himself and peeped out through the shutters. According to legend the 'peeping Tom' was then struck blind. Lady Godiva was a real person, but the story is probably only just that.

To **Plug A Song** or **Book** is to promote it and make as many people aware of it as possible. In the early part of the 20th century Radio Normandie was one of the first independent stations and was broadcast from northern France. Radio Normandie was also the first commercial radio station to transmit to England during the 1930s and one of their sources of income was to receive payments to play records and promote them throughout the country. The station's founder and main broadcaster was a Captain Leonard Plugge, which was probably how the phrase originated.

A **Private Eye** is a private investigator. Some people assume the 'eye' is short for 'investigator', but the real origin is a visual one. In 1850 Allan Pinkerton opened America's first detective agency in Chicago. Pinkerton was Scottish but played a large part in American history by preventing an assassination attempt on Abraham Lincoln and by organizing the first official Secret Service tour of duty behind Confederate lines during the War for Southern Independence. He rode with lawmen along the Old Frontier and hunted down members of Jesse James's gang, Butch Cassidy, the Reno brothers and the Hole in the Wall Gang. The

Pinkerton National Detective Agency used the slogan 'We Never Sleep' for its advertising and the accompanying logo depicted a large, wide-open eye. Pinkerton himself gained fame by being known simply as 'The Eye'. The phrase travelled to Britain during the 1930s with the early detective movies and it soon became an established part of our everyday language. The agency still exists.

The expression **Standing On The Shoulders Of Giants** is a tribute paid by an achiever to those who went before and whose research benefited the final results. Noel Gallagher named Oasis's fourth studio album *Standing on the Shoulder of Giants* after noticing the idiom engraved onto the side of a £2 coin. **On the Shoulders of Giants** is also the title of a collection of works by the major scientists Johannes Kepler, Galileo Galilei, Isaac Newton, Albert Einstein and Nicolaus Copernicus, compiled and edited by Stephen Hawking.

It is often thought the origin of the expression goes back to Isaac Newton, who famously wrote, in a letter to his great rival Robert Hooke on 5 February 1676, that 'What Des-Cartes did was a good step. You have added much in several ways and especially in taking the colours of these plates

169

into philosophical consideration. If I have seen a little further it is only by standing on the shoulders of Giants.' Newton was clearly accepting the great work carried out by other scientists both before and during his time that had a major part in the success he himself had achieved as a scientist.

But Newton's was not an original reference. In 1159 the author John of Salisbury wrote of Bernard of Chartres in his book, *Metalogicon*:

> Bernard of Chartres used to say that we are like dwarfs on the shoulders of giants, so that we can see more than they, and see things at a greater distance, not by virtue of any sharpness of sight on our part, or any physical distinction, but because we are carried high and raised up by their giant stature.

Sweet FA does not stand for Sweet Fuck All, as many people believe. In fact, it stands for Sweet Fanny Adams. Fanny was an eight-year-old girl living in Alton, Hampshire, who was found murdered, her body cut into pieces and thrown into the River Wey. At around the same time the English Navy changed their rations from salted tack to low-grade tins of chopped-up sweet mutton. The new ration was both tasteless and unpopular, and with macabre humour sailors suggested the new meat was the remains of the murdered girl and christened the ration 'Sweet Fanny Adams'. On land the phrase was adopted to describe anything boring, monotonous and not worth describing (as was the ration and not poor Fanny) hence 'Sweet FA'.

To **Wash Your Dirty Linen In Public** is a phrase used when a person reveals something personally unpleasant that would have been far better kept private. Although it is a fairly obvious idiom it does have an interesting origin.

When Napoleon returned from his first period of exile on the island of Elba, near Italy, he was asked about his experience. 'It is at home and not in public that one washes ones dirty linen,' he replied. Napoleon had been sent to Elba after his forced abdication as a result of the Treaty of Fontainebleau. Arriving there on 4 May 1814, he was made emperor of the island and allowed to keep a personal guard of six hundred men. Despite being surrounded by the British navy, the emperor somehow managed to escape back to

France where he again took control on 26 February 1815. Four months later his army was crushed at Waterloo and Napoleon was again exiled, this time to the far more isolated island of St Helena in the South Atlantic. That time there was to be no escape, and no more dirty laundry.

10: POLITICS

In The Bag is a phrase used to describe something of an absolute certain outcome. Since the beginning of the English Parliament, tradition has it that all petitions brought before the House of Commons, which had a successful outcome, would be placed by the Speaker in a large velvet bag hung from the back of the Speaker's chair. Therefore politicians, or reporters, describing a petition as 'in the bag' would be confirming its favourable outcome. The bag, although now only symbolic, still hangs behind the Speaker's chair.

To **Jump On The Bandwagon** means to join in, often uninvited, an already successful venture and gain some sort of self-benefit. In the Deep South of America travelling bands would once perform on their wagons in front of political or other rallies. Usually the bands would be a highlight of an event, attracting the largest crowds, so it was common for political or religious leaders to climb up on to the wagon, interrupting the music (sometimes with prior agreement) and gain themselves an immediate captive audience. Crowds would often tolerate this knowing the musicians would be back in due course. The practice had continued for over a hundred years before it was first recorded during William Jennings Bryan's presidential campaign in the early 1900s.

A **Battle Axe** is a comic, if not offensive, term for belligerent and stubborn old woman. Its origins can be found in America and the early years of the women's rights movement. The phrase itself was originally meant as a rallying or war cry but backfired when the movement published a journal called *The Battle Axe* (to signify their resolve). Instead, the phrase was quickly used as a derogatory term for the domineering and hostile nature of the majority involved in that movement and as a reflection of what many, including less aggressive women, thought of its members.

Beyond The Pale is usually applied to someone who has committed an unspeakable act or behaves immorally. A Pale, historically, is an area around a town or a city, which was subject to a particular jurisdiction and was governed by the King or one of his lords. Areas outside the Pale were generally regarded as lawless and uncouth, so unaccountable peasants of medieval England, Ireland and France (the English-held towns of Calais and Dublin established their own Pales) were regarded by relatively civilised town-folk as from 'Beyond the Pale'.

Bob's Your Uncle is often used to describe something that is resolved in your favour without much effort, such as 'Just send the form in and Bob's your uncle'. The phrase was in regular use in Britain from the 1890s and comes from the promotion in 1886 of Arthur Balfour to Secretary of State for Ireland. Balfour was a surprise choice for the position and few regarded him as qualified for the post. But when it became known he was the nephew of Prime Minister Robert Gascoyne-

Cecil, Third Marquis of Salisbury, the joke circulated that, if Robert was your uncle, a deed was as good as done.

Hear Hear is often used in political circles to suggest agreement or endorsement of something being said. Originally any disagreement with a speaker, either in the Commons or the House of Lords, would be expressed by loud humming from those with opposing views, in an attempt to drown out the speech being made. But members agreeing and in favour of the speaker would call for those humming to listen by shouting 'hear him, hear him'. This phrase has evolved over the years to the one used today.

When somebody is told to **Toe The Line**, they are expected to follow the rules and submit to authority. Originally this phrase refers to the lines drawn along the two front benches in the House of Commons which still exists. The two lines are strategically placed at a distance far enough apart to prevent opposing members reaching each other with their swords, should the debating become heated enough. Any member becoming animated enough during an argument to step over a line would be called to order and told to 'toe the line'. Tradition still prevents members from 'crossing the line' but these days none of them carries swords or other weapons, although it would be much more fun if they did.

It is no surprise to find the Americans claiming the origin of this historic British tradition. The US Navy website states, 'The space between each pair of deck planks in a wooden ship was filled with a packing material called "oakum" and then sealed with a mixture of pitch and tar. The result, from afar, was a series of parallel lines a half-foot or so apart, running the length of the deck. Once a week, usually on Sunday, a warship's crew was ordered to fall in at quarters with each group of men into which the crew was divided and lined up in formation in a given area of the deck. To ensure the neat alignment of each row the sailors were directed to stand with their toes just touching a particular seam.' Also, a naval punishment for boys too young to be flogged was to stand for hours on end in any weather with their toes touching the line. If they moved their punishment would be extended.

When an idea is **Pie In The Sky** it is thought to be a good idea but unlikely to amount to a successful conclusion, especially for the person suggesting the plan. The original use of the phrase was, in fact, quite cynical. It comes from a trade union parody often used during the years of the Great Depression early in the 20th century. The hymn, entitled 'The Sweet By And By', goes like this: 'You will eat, bye and bye / In that glorious land above the sky / work and pray, live on hay / You'll get pie in the sky when you die.' And through that popular movement the phrase passed over into wider use.

A **Spin Doctor** is a person who has the task of controlling the public image of a person or organization. Governments, for example, or most political organizations seem to be no longer able to function without employing spin doctors to present their views and decisions to the world at large. Essentially little more than public relations employees, these types wield the kind of power and influence their paymasters can only wish for. Alistair Campbell, for example, was the spin doctor for Tony Blair's Labour government during the late 1990s and early 2000s and it was his job to make Tony Blair and his policies look good to the British public. Not an easy task.

The expression originated in America in the early 1980s when Ronald Reagan described public relations advisers to his Star Wars Defence Initiative (SDI) as being on 'spin control'. Reagan, an avid baseball fan, knew that spin placed on the ball by a pitcher was designed to fool the batsman, and he used the expression to describe his PR advisers' work to provide a preferred interpretation of events to the world's media. Those manipulating the 'spin control' became known as the spin doctors, an expression picked up by British journalists and used to describe the purveyors of shady tactics or, as some put it, benders of the truth.

When It Comes To The Crunch is an expression used to explain a decisive moment or perhaps an epiphany determining a future course. The word 'crunch' was first used in this sense by Sir Winston Churchill during the build-up to, and during the course of, the Second World War. The great man regularly used the expression to describe challenging situations. For example the *Daily Telegraph* quoted him in 1939, at the close of the

Spanish Civil War: 'Whether Spain will be allowed to find its way back to sanity and health depends upon the general adjustment or outcome of the European crunch.' By that he was referring to the wider problem of the German Nazi Party and their intentions towards Europe as a whole. Churchill, a lucid speaker and inventive writer, often used creative language to emphasise a point or two.

11: THE LAW

A **Baker's Dozen** is 13, not 12. There are two established theories as to the origin of the phrase. The first is set in medieval England and identifies the sales techniques of tradesmen such as bakers and fishmongers. When selling directly to the public, merchants would have a fixed price for their wares. But when selling to bulk buyers such as town market stall-holders the merchant would gift an extra item for every dozen bought. In such cases the 13th loaf or fish would represent the stall-holder's profit on the items he buys and then sells at market.

The second theory dates back to the 13th century when bakers had the reputation of selling underweight loaves, although sometimes unfairly as the baking process sometimes made the bread 'thin' on the inside. In 1266 regulations were brought in to standardise weights of various loaves and the penalty for being underweight could mean a day in the stocks. To avoid this, bakers began to add an extra loaf, known as a vantage loaf, to every dozen sold, to make sure they stayed within the new laws.

A **Barrack Room Lawyer** is a derogatory term meaning they are unqualified or inexperienced at what they are attempting to achieve (usually in professional circles). Since the 19th century the Queen's (or King's) Regulations have enabled soldiers without any formal legal training to conduct their own defence, make a formal complaint to superiors or promote their own interests. But those who did so were held in contempt by their commanding officers, who bestowed the uncomplimentary tag upon them. The phrase had passed into common usage by the beginning of the 20th century.

If we **Have A Beef** it usually means we have something to moan about or a quarrel to pick.

The earliest record of the phrase is found in the 1811 *Dictionary Of The Vulgar Tongue*, which suggests to 'cry beef' meant to give the alarm. Prior to that, in criminal London, it was known that the traditional cry of 'stop thief' was mocked and drowned out by passing fellow criminals who loudly called 'hot beef' instead, in a bid to confuse law-abiding passers-by and allow their colleague to make his getaway.

To suggest somebody has a **Brass Neck** is to imply they have some nerve and will try anything to suit their own purposes, usually with the reluctant admiration of others for their cheek. The origin of this phrase appears to lie with the legend of a highwayman who was sentenced to hang from a tree for his crimes. This method of hanging brought about a slow death by choking so the highwayman came up with a cunning plan. He would swallow a piece of brass tube, with a wire attached to it and held inside his mouth, in the hope this would prevent his throat being crushed and allow him to breathe long enough for the crowd to disperse. All he then needed was an accomplice who could cut him down, remove the tube and save

183

his life. Unfortunately it is not known if this is actually true (I hope it is) but the legend is certainly where the term 'brass neck' came from.

To be thrown in **The Clink** means to be locked away in jail. It is sometimes thought the clink is a reference to the sound of the irons and chains placed on a convict. In fact, The Clink is the name of one of the oldest prisons in England, located in the London borough of Southwark since the 13th century. The Liberty Of Clink was the name of the district in which the prison was located; it was south of the river and exempt from the jurisdiction of the City of London. In other words, it could make up its own rules. Originally owned by the Bishop of Winchester, The Clink had a fearsome reputation with punishments including boiling in oil, the rack, breaking on the wheel, being forced to stand in cold water until a prisoner's feet rotted, being slowly crushed under weights and starvation. The only way to avoid such treatment was to pay bribes and therefore The Clink provided a vast source of income for the Church from those prisoners on the receiving end of its barbaric practices. Finally destroyed by rioters in 1780, The Clink is now a museum, built on the foundations of the original building and a fitting reminder of London life throughout the Middle Ages.

A **Hijack** is usually associated with the forced or violent theft of a mode of transport, normally aircraft. But it is also often applied to a person taking over any proceedings that have already begun. The earliest reference to its origin can be traced to the old English highwaymen who would steal coaches at musket point and traditionally used the words 'Hold 'em high, Jack', meaning everybody on the coach had to hold their hands in the air while he took control.

By Hook Or By Crook is an expression we use to explain achieving something by any means possible, either honestly or otherwise. For its origin we need to know that a hook is a blunt billhook and a crook is a curved shaft a shepherd uses to gather his flock. In medieval feudal England a law was passed preventing the cutting down of trees or lopping of branches in order to gather firewood. But the law permitted the poor to gather dead wood from forests and deemed anything they could collect with a blunt hook or shepherd's crook was allowable. The Bodmin Register of 1525 states, 'Dynmure Wood is open to the inhabitants of Bodmin... to bear away on their backs a burden of lop, hook, crook and bag wood.'

An **Ignoramus** is somebody of low intelligence and who applies little or no thought to a situation. Much of our legal language derives from Latin and many modern terms of law can be traced to the original use of that language. In Latin 'ignoramus' means 'we don't know [why this case was brought]' and the word would traditionally be stamped on legal documents rejected by the courts as badly thought-out and without basis. The expression has been in general use since George Ruggle wrote a play in 1615 called *Ignoramus* in which the title character, a lawyer, demonstrated the ignorance of the common lawyers of that time.

A **Laughing Stock** is a person exposed to a wide number of other people for their stupidity. In medieval England the stocks were used in many villages to hold a petty criminal or daft soul who had been caught doing something silly, in front of their own community. Their hands and feet would be secured in the wooden frame and the village folk would gather round to laugh at and humiliate the hapless person, often by pelting them with rotten vegetables.

To be pushed from **Pillar To Post** means to be in a constant state of flux and probably harassed at the same time. In the Middle Ages each town and village in England had both a pillory and a whipping post. A pillory (also known as the stocks) was a place where petty criminals or traders who had swindled their customers would be clamped by their head and arms, and local people would gather round to humiliate them. In the case of a more serious crime, offenders would first be put in the pillory and then taken to the whipping post, being jostled along the way, for a public flogging. So the phrase began as 'from the pillory to the post' but evolved into the idiom we use these days.

The phrase **Possession Is Nine Tenths Of The Law** began life as Possession Is Nine Points Of The Law. The phrase was used by anybody claiming an advantage in a legal situation, especially over the ownership of property, whether it belonged to them or not. Prior to the 17th century the expression was 11 out of 12 and it is not known why it was later reduced. However, the nine points are: patience, money, a just cause, a good lawyer, good counsel, witnesses, a true jury, a good judge and good luck.

To **Read The Riot Act** is an expression used when an individual or group of people are given a severe rollicking about their bad behaviour. The original Riot Act was passed by the British government in 1715 as an attempt to increase the powers of the civil authorities when a town was threatened by riotous behaviour. The Act made it a serious crime for groups of 12 or more people not to disperse within one hour of it being read out to the mob.

The Act read: 'Our Sovereign Lord the King chargeth and commandeth all persons being assembled immediately to disperse themselves, and peaceably to depart to their habitations or to their lawful business, upon the pains contained in the Act made in the first year of King George for preventing tumultuous and riotous assemblies. God save the King.'

Those failing to disperse risked penal servitude for not less than three years or imprisonment with hard labour for up to two years. Actually reading it out took extraordinary courage and often, during serious disturbances, many didn't hear it anyway.

After the infamous Peterloo Massacre near Manchester in 1819 many of the convicted demonstrators claimed not to have heard the Act being read and the same defence was put during trials for the 1743 Gin Riots, 1768 St George's Massacre and the 1780 Gordon Riots. The Act remained on the statute book until the 1970s, but little use had been made of it for over a century, apart from when I come home late from the pub, singing loudly.

To be **Caught Red Handed** is to be caught in the process of committing a crime. The expression 'redhand' used to be an official Scottish legal phrase meaning to be caught in the act. The great poet and novelist Sir Walter Scott (1771–1832) is generally regarded as responsible for bringing it into wider use.

There is another possible origin from Ulster, where the Red Hand of Ulster is a symbol that forms part of the flag of Northern Ireland. Its origin is uncertain but, according to one well-known myth, it comes from a story relating to a time when Ulster had no rightful heir. The people agreed that a boat race should be held across one of the lakes and that 'whosoever's hand is the first to touch the shore of Ulster, so he shall be made the king.' One of the challengers loved Ulster so much his desire to rule led him to cut off his hand and throw it to the shore in an attempt to win. It was said that the blood on his other hand led to the symbol of Ulster.

Rigmarole is an unusual word with an interesting origin. It is used to describe something disconnected, rambling and difficult to see a way through. It is now well over 700 years old and dates back to 1291 when the Scottish noblemen signed a deed of loyalty to King Edward I of England. Each of them fixed their seal to it and when all the attachments were joined together and presented to the King it was 40ft long. The deeds were known as the Ragman Roll and it was a dishevelled mix and match of all the Scottish deeds, both confusing and complicated. Ragman Roll morphed into 'Rigmarole' and became used to describe anything of a troublesome, time-consuming and awkward nature.

If something **Rings True**, or has the **Ring Of Truth** to it, it is generally thought to be the genuine article, despite possible alternatives. Centuries ago, coins of the realm were made of pure metals instead of the hard-wearing alloy that makes up modern currency. But pure metals such as silver have a sonorous ring to them when dropped on a hard counter, so it was quite possible to tell the difference between a genuine coin and a counterfeit by the ringing sound it made when tested.

To Be Screwed is a widely used term for being cheated, or placed at a disadvantage. During the 19th century English prisons were intended to be cruel places of punishment (hard labour) to deter prisoners from returning. One of these forms of punishment was to force a convict to turn a crank handle up to 10,000 times a day. These handles were designed in a way that the hard labour could be made even worse by a warder turning a simple screw, which increased the resistance of the handle. In such barbaric places, bribery and corruption were commonplace and any prisoner who did not agree to a warder's demands could find himself being 'screwed' the next time he was on the handle.

A **Soap Opera** has become the accepted term for a regular radio, and later TV, drama shows usually based around normal life. Each episode ends in suspense to ensure listeners and viewers return to find out what happens next. The origin of the phrase lies in America during the 1920s with a popular weekly radio programme called *Amos And Andy*. As the show was always broadcast during prime time, and for family viewing, the soap manufacturers Proctor and Gamble started to advertise their products during the breaks and later sponsored the programme. Soon afterwards other similar shows (and soap manufacturers) followed suit and a critic, writing in 1938, began referring to them generally as 'soaps'. The word 'opera' was then borrowed from the popular 'horse operas' (a term for cowboy films) of the 1930s.

On The Treadmill is another saying relating to Victorian hard labour, one the great writer Oscar Wilde was subjected to during his prison sentence in the late 1800s. Today it is used to describe exhausting, never-ending work that is usually without even acknowledgement. In Oscar's day a treadmill was a primitive version of modern-day step machines found in every gym or fitness centre. It was a row of evenly spaced wooden planks joined at each end by a large round cog. Poor Oscar and his fellow convicts were forced to walk the treadmill all day long, akin to walking up an endless staircase but without actually leaving the bottom step. As the playwright himself said at the time, 'If this is the way the Queen treats her prisoners, she doesn't deserve to have any.' Needless to say none of his clothes still fitted when he eventually left Reading Gaol. And today, in fitness centres, they all pay to do it.

When something has **Gone West** it is generally lost forever. Usually it is a plan, project or perhaps business deal that 'goes west' when something major goes wrong. There is a suggestion that the sun setting in the west may be the root of the phrase but it is more likely to be the Tyburn gibbet, a place of execution once situated near the site of Marble Arch in central London, where we uncover the secret. London's main prisons at either Newgate or **The Clink** were both located on the east side of the city and a condemned man would be loaded on to a cart and taken west to meet his fate. Nobody ever returned from the journey west.

12: MUSIC, THEATRE AND PERFORMANCE

A **Blonde Bombshell** is a cliché now used to describe any dynamic or attractive blonde lady, usually a singer, actress or film star but often applied to politicians or business figures. The original 'Blonde Bombshell' was Jean Harlow, an American actress, mistress of the one-line witticism and star of the 1933 film *Bombshell*. When the film was later released in the UK producers, worried it might be perceived as a war film, changed its title to *Blonde Bombshell* and the phrase immediately passed into the English language.

To hope somebody **Breaks A Leg** is in fact a message of goodwill and good luck, usually reserved for a stage actor or musician prior to a performance. Some claim the expression originates from the assassination of President Abraham Lincoln who was shot dead in his private box at Ford's Theater in Washington DC, on 14 April 1865. His murderer John Wilkes Booth, a renowned Shakespearean actor, broke his leg jumping down on to the stage to make his escape. The claim is that the saying arose as a form of black humour in relation to that event. But in fact the phrase was known centuries before that when a measure of the success of a stage performance was the number of times an audience called the performers back to the front of the stage for applause. Each time the curtain was reopened the actors bowed or curtsied, and the more often that happened the greater the chance of 'breaking a leg'.

That **Old Chestnut** is a phrase used to describe an old joke or excuse, something that has been heard many times before. The origin of the saying dates back to 1816 when the play *The Broken Sword* by William Diamond was staged in Covent Garden, London. One of the play's characters, Captain

Xavier, often repeats the same joke about a cork tree, with slight variations each time. At one point another character, Pablo, interrupts with the punchline and says, 'It's a chestnut. I have heard you tell the joke 27 times and it's a chestnut.' At some point later American actor William Warren was playing the part of Pablo and while he was being entertained at a society dinner one evening, another guest began to recite an old, well-known joke. Warren interrupted and said with a flourish, 'It's an old chestnut, that's what it is,' much to the amusement of everybody there. That is how the expression passed into the English language.

Cold Comfort is little comfort at all, usually only offering minor encouragement in the face of adversity. The phrase was popularized by Shakespeare, who included in his play *The Taming of the Shrew* (Act 4 Scene i) the lines: 'But wilt thou make a fire, or shall I complain on thee to our mistress, whose hand, she being now at hand, thou shalt soon feel, to thy cold comfort, for being slow in thy hot office?' But an earlier example can be found in literature during the 14th century when E.E. Allit wrote, 'My Lorde! Colde watz his own comforte.'

197

Putting The Dampers on something means to discourage or to tone down the enthusiasm somebody is showing for an idea. This saying has a musical origin and relates to the piano. A damper is operated by a foot pedal, which presses it against the strings to reduce the instrument's sound. To 'put the dampers' on a concert performance was a phrase used to describe toning the sound of the orchestra down.

To have **Egg On Your Face** implies a decision or choice has been made which later turns out to be a mistake, leaving a person looking foolish. Some suggest this is a relatively recent phrase and originates in America during the election campaigns of the 1960s and 1970s. At the time it was common for opponents of a candidate to throw eggs at them in order to make them look foolish. There is, however, strong evidence to suggest the Victorian theatres hold the real origin. At the time, during the slapstick comedies of the era, the fall guy would usually have eggs broken on his forehead to make him look foolish, not unlike taking a custard pie in the face. Those crazy Victorians!

198

To **Face The Music** has two possible origins. The first is that nervous (often terrified) actors and actresses, on an opening night, would have to go out on stage at the start of their performance and quite literally 'face the music' (as the orchestra pit sat directly in front of the stage with the musician facing the actors). In this case 'facing the music' meant the actor actually went out and performed, rather than **losing their bottle** (their nerve). The second explanation suggests that a dishonourable military discharge would always result in the disgraced serviceman being marched off barracks to the sound of drummers playing (being 'drummed out'), in which case he too had 'faced the music'.

As Fit As A Fiddle is used to indicate a person or an animal is in good condition, lively and energetic. But since its origin we seem to have lost a letter along the way. Back in the days of medieval court the fittest person was thought to be the fiddler as they danced and scampered about as they played their music throughout the crowds. The phrase widely used at the time was 'as fit as a fiddler', which makes a lot more sense.

The **Green Eyed Monster** is a beast to be avoided and can affect either sex of any age group. It is the ugliest and most destructive of all emotions – jealousy. Usually, green is the colour associated with illness and that is because it is the colour of unripe fruit or vegetables that can cause stomach cramps and sickness. To find out how we associate it with jealousy we turn to Shakespeare's *The Merchant of Venice* (1600) and Portia's lines:

How all the other passions fleet to air,
As doubtful thoughts and rash-embraced despair,
And shuddering fear, and green-eyed jealousy
Oh love, be moderate and allay thy ecstasy,
In measure rein thy joy; scant this excess.
I feel too much thy blessing: make it less,
For fear I surfeit.

A few years later, the playwright used the expression again when he wrote in *Othello*:

Oh, beware, my lord, of jealousy;
It is the green-eyed monster which doth mock
The meat it feeds on; that cuckold lives in bliss
Who, certain of his fate, loves not his wronger;
But, oh what damned minutes tells he o'er

Who dotes, yet doubts, suspects, yet
strongly loves!

To indulge in **Horseplay** is to behave in a
boisterous but friendly manner. The origin of this
saying lies with the English Morris dancers. At
country fairs players riding wooden hobbyhorses
usually accompanied Morris dancers. These
'horses' were expected to engage in wild and
uncontrollable antics to entertain the crowds,
much as a clown does in a circus, and the
'horseplay' became a popular and important part
of the Morris dancers' act.

Jumping The Shark is a phrase used to describe
good television shows that have run out of steam
and become average at best. This has been the
case with many classic comedies, which run for
one series too many and standards and ratings
start to fall. One of the great TV shows of the
1970s was *Happy Days*, featuring The Fonz, the
Cunningham family and their friends. All of
America and Britain seemed captivated by the
show until the writing became tired, and during
the last series viewers started to switch off. The
final straw seems to have been a scene in which

The Fonz (Henry Winkler) was waterskiing in his leather jacket and motorcycle boots and literally jumped over a shark. For many critics enough was enough and that scene marked the end for the show, though not of its well-earned cult status.

To **Make Someone An Offer They Cannot Refuse** is an expression used the world over but it is a surprisingly recent one. It was Mario Puzo who coined the phrase, in his classic 1969 novel, *The Godfather*. In the movie it is delivered by Marlon Brando in the following exchange:

Clemenza: His family is out of the house. Fanucci's alone in the cafe.
Tessio: Vito, here's my $50. Buona fortuna [good luck].
Clemenza: Hey Vito, are you sure he's going to go for it?
Vito: I will make an offer he don't refuse. Don't worry.

When something is **On The Nose** we take it to be right on time, exact and precise. The reason this phrase is used can be found in the studios of the very early live radio broadcasts where a programme producer would signal to the performers in the sound-proofed booths when they went 'on air and live' by touching his nose.

Some think it that the expression **I'm Over the Moon** has only existed since the 1970s, when it was first used by footballers and match commentators to describe euphoria at a favourable result. The nursery rhyme which starts 'Hey diddle diddle, the cat and the fiddle, the cow jumped over the moon' has been popular since 1765 and is often thought to be the origin of the phrase. But its origin can be found as early as 1696 and Sir John Vanbrugh's play The Relapse, during which one character, Hoyden, says, 'Oh Lord, I could leap over the moon' to express his delight.

In 1857, an entry can be found in the diaries of Lady Cavendish that recorded that her siblings were 'over the moon' at the news of a new arrival to their family. Also in the 19th century, it is said that Prime Minister William Gladstone and his wife used to have their own language full of idioms, including this one. The eighth Duke of Cavendish played a leading role in the Gladstone governments and the two families were known to be close, so there is an obvious connection there.

The expression was also popular with a group of Victorian dandies and writers who used 'over the moon' to express complete happiness.

But it was England's World Cup winning manager Sir Alf Ramsey who made the phrase popular. In 1962 he was interviewed directly after a successful England match and declared that he was 'over the moon with the performance'. This remark travelled the globe in print, radio and television formats and is the reason it became so well known, especially throughout football circles, which is home to myriad clichés.

To **Play It By Ear** means to take a situation as we find it and then adapt our actions as we have to. In other words to wait and see what happens before reacting. This is a musical expression and can be traced back to the time prior to recording equipment. In those days composers and songwriters had to craft out a piece of music on a piano, and write it down as they went along to remember how the melody went. Musicians also had to listen to one or two instruments and then pick out their parts by ear, which was known as 'playing it by ear'. These days musicians who can play their part just by listening to a record are said to be 'playing it by ear', but that is a lot easier now than it used to be.

To **Play Second Fiddle** is to have a supporting role to a more dominant character. In an orchestra the string quartet plays an important role in the overall melody and sound that is created. Whilst the lead fiddler concentrates on the actual melody of a piece of music, the second fiddler supports the sound by playing a harmony to the first. Although equally important, it tends to be noticed far less than the first fiddler's musical contribution.

To **Pull Out All The Stops** implies a big, concerted effort is being made to complete a task in time. This is a simple one and alludes to the grand church organs, which used 'stops' to tone down the volume of the instrument. At vast gatherings, with many people present, an organist would 'pull out the stops' to increase the sound of his organ, enabling everybody at the back to hear it clearly.

Living The Life Of Reilly is one of the strangest sayings of all. It suggests that the person referred to lives a charmed life of ease, and anyone blessed with good fortune is considered to be doing the same. The origin of the phrase is unclear, but it could perhaps lie with the earliest recorded reference, which is found in a song called 'My Name Is Kelly', written by H Pearse in 1919. It was a popular music hall song and included the lines 'Faith and my name is Kelly, Michael Kelly, but I'm living the life of Reilly just the same.' This lyric is a reference to an earlier song performed in the music halls during the 1880s, which described a character called O'Reilly who was a working-class Irish immigrant. He always claimed to be on the verge of hitting the big time, making himself and everyone around him rich in the process.

If you ask somebody to **Put A Sock In It**, you are asking them to quieten down. In the early days of sound recording and radio broadcasting, the ability to control instrument volumes was severely limited, but orchestras and bands, the forerunners of the modern pop band, were in high demand. Usually the horn sections would drown out the wind instruments and strings in the enclosed studios. In an attempt to even the sound out, horn players muffled their instruments by literally stuffing a sock into the mouth of their instruments, bringing them down to the same sound level as the rest of the band.

To be **As Snug As A Bug In A Rug** is a nice, warm and comfortable place to be. In your favourite armchair with a favourite rug around your shoulders is a good example.

Wednesday 6 September 1769 saw Stratford-upon-Avon play host to an important event: the first three-day Shakespeare Festival, commemorating the life and works of the great playwright. During the festival the celebrated actor and playwright David Garrick performed his own comedy, or farce, entitled The Stratford Jubilee, which was a huge success and later performed in London's West End. One of Garrick's most popular and inventive lines in the script was: 'If she [a wealthy widow] has the mopus [old English word for money] then I'll have her as snug as a bug in a rug.' It was a typical play on the rhythm and rhyme of words that caught the public's imagination and became part of our common language.

Garrick was such an influential figure at the time that he was remembered long after his death in 1779. In 1831 a gentleman's club was founded in London by a group of literary gentlemen who described it as a place where 'actors and men of refinement and education might meet on equal terms', where 'patrons of the drama and its professors were to be brought together', and where 'easy intercourse was to be promoted between artists and patrons.' The Garrick Club was thus named in his honour. Likewise, the Garrick Theatre in London, opened on 24 April 1889, was also named after the popular actor.

Back To Square One means back to the beginning. The origin of the phrase is easily traced to the 1930s when commentary on football matches began to be broadcast by the BBC. The BBC's schedule magazine, *The Radio Times*, devised a numbered grid system which they published enabling commentators to indicate to listeners exactly where the ball was on the pitch. Square one was the goalkeeper's area and whenever the ball was passed back to him, signalling the start of the forward movement of the team, play was referred to as being 'back to square one'.

When someone **Steals Your Thunder** they are taking credit for something that you should properly be credited for. The phrase was in regular use by 1900, especially by jealous politicians claiming their brilliant and original ideas had been stolen by another. The expression was coined in the early 1700s by the playwright and critic John Dennis, who discovered the sound of thunder could be reproduced to great effect by pummelling large tin sheets backstage at the Drury Lane Theatre in London. At a time when sound effects were virtually unheard of, his idea considerably added to the drama and drew much attention. His play, on the other hand, did not attract attention and was replaced by *Macbeth* in a matter of weeks. Shortly afterwards the embittered Dennis saw a performance of *Macbeth* and was furious to hear his thunder being reproduced without his permission. Writing a review the following day, he raged, 'See what rascals they are. They will not run my play and yet they steal my thunder.'

If you have achieved something **On A Wing And A Prayer** then you have been very lucky to achieve it at all. It has been managed with all the odds having been stacked against it, and without explanation. We can also hope to achieve something on a wing and a prayer when we are not feeling too hopeful.

The origin of this expression can be traced to a patriotic Second World War song written by Jimmie McHugh and Harold Adamson that became popular in 1943. The song tells the tale of a fighter pilot nursing his damaged aircraft back to England on only one engine. The chorus line read:

Comin' in on a wing and a prayer
Comin' in on a wing and a prayer
Though there's one motor gone
We can still carry on
Comin' in on a wing and a prayer

The song was based upon the actual words a pilot radioed from his stricken aircraft to ground control as he prepared to land after a bombing mission. It was soon so popular that the expression became a firm part of the English language, regularly being used as newspaper headlines for stories about bravery and heroism. The following year Hollywood made a war film called *Wing and a Prayer* about the heroic crew of an American carrier during the early days of the Second World War (early days for the Americans, that is) in the Pacific Theatre. Essentially a propaganda film, it nevertheless proved so popular it was nominated for an Academy Award for Best Original Screenplay.

McHugh and Adamson wrote many uplifting patriotic songs during the war and were eventually awarded the Presidential Certificate of Merit by President Harry Truman.

A similar phrase, **Winging It**, is thought by some to be connected, but in fact this is a theatrical term, used to describe a stand-in actor who is having to learn his or her part in the wings of a theatre before and between stage appearances.

13: THE USA

If we are **Barking Up The Wrong Tree** we have misunderstood something and are now pursuing the wrong course of action. This is a phrase of north American origin and comes from the old practice of racoon-hunting dating back to the 1800s. Racoons are nocturnal animals and hunters would roam around the forests in darkness, using dogs to pick up a scent. Frightened racoons would scurry to safety in the branches of trees but hunting dogs would stand with their paws on the base of a trunk barking. A hunter would then climb the tree for the catch, but would sometimes find the racoon nowhere to be seen. When that happened it was said the dog had been 'barking up the wrong tree'.

Bootleggers are well known for selling items, originally alcohol, without proper permission and avoiding tax or other duties, making them cheaper and therefore popular. These days a bootlegger is better known for making copies of music or films and selling them without the artist's or producer's permission and without paying any royalties due. The expression was first recorded in the mid-1800s and applied to those who sold illegal liquor to Indians in the Far West. Those making the sales would ride out to the reservations with thin bottles of alcohol concealed in their riding boots and quickly became known by the authorities as 'bootleggers'. The phrase travelled across the sea to the UK and was soon applied to anyone involved in counterfeit activity.

If we are **On The Breadline** we are poor and on the verge of destitution, the inference being very close to disaster. This is an American phrase, which travelled across the Atlantic in the 1870s. Around that time a celebrated bakery, run by the Fleischman family in New York, was famous for the quality and freshness of its bread. The reason was that all the bread was baked in the morning and any left over at the end of each day was given to the poor and starving for free, rather than kept for the following day's customers. A queue, in America, is known as a line, so at the end of each day a 'breadline' would form outside the premises, and those on it were close to starvation.

A **Bucket Shop** is a place to buy cheap tickets, usually airline or theatre tickets. But, before that term was coined, such places were usually illegal brokerage houses that cheated their customers. The original 'bucket shops' were seedy American bars where patrons could buy cheap beer by the bucketful and these bars often cheated their customers who had no way of measuring out the amount of beer in the bucket, other than by the glass. By the time they had drunk the bucketful, customers had, more often than not, lost their senses, their bearings, the use of their legs and, more importantly for the innkeeper, count.

Someone is said to have a **Chip On Their Shoulder** when they are looking for an argument for no apparent reason, at least not one that is obvious to anyone else. Its origin can be found 200 years ago, in a custom used by American schoolboys to challenge each other to a fight. One would place a twig or piece of bark (a chip of wood) on his shoulder and challenge another to knock it off. If he did a fight started. Then, as now, it is a phrase used to describe someone who is spoiling for a row.

Being on **Cloud Nine** describes a feeling of total happiness and content, or euphoria. Between the 1930s and 1950s the American Weather Bureau divided clouds into classes numbered one to nine. The highest, cloud nine, is the cumulonimbus, which reaches 40,000ft and can appear as white mountains, even on a sunny day. During the 1950s a popular US radio show, *Johnny Dollar*, ran an episode during which the hero was often knocked unconscious and then transported to 'cloud nine' where he was revived and lived to be a hero again in other episodes. It was through that association that 'cloud nine' passed into the English language as a popular phrase for the peak of existence.

A **Deadline** is the final date or time by which a task has to be completed. Originally the deadline was a white line painted at Andersonville prisoner of war camp in America during the American Civil War. Without the use of wire and fencing Andersonville simply had marksmen placed around the perimeter and any prisoner crossing the white line was shot dead, no questions asked. Since then the phrase has been applied to newspaper writers who had to have their article submitted by a certain time before a publication went to print. If they missed the deadline their story was considered dead as it would be out of date by the following day's print run.

To say somebody is **Dressed To Kill** is to suggest they are smart, fashionable and set to make a romantic conquest. The origin of this phrase appears to have come from the *Cambridge Tribune*, an American newspaper. On 10 November 1881 an army recruit, resplendent in his new shiny uniform, was asked how he felt about his appearance. Unimpressed by either the splendour or the question, the soldier simply replied to the interviewer 'I am dressed to kill'.

If something is described as **Fair To Middling**, it is generally accepted as being around average, or just above. The phrase was originally used in the American cotton industry in the mid-1800s. Commercial cotton was graded in categories ranging between inferior and fine. Average was known as 'middling' and just above it the grade was called 'fair'. The term was in wide-ranging use across the water by 1837 and in October of that year the *Southern Literary Messenger* of Richmond, Virginia, reported the following: 'A dinner on the Plains, Tuesday September 20th – given at the country seat of JC Jones, Esq for the officers of the Peacock and Enterprise. The viands [items of food] were fair to middling.' In England the phrase was first listed in the *Century Dictionary* of 1889 as meaning 'moderately good'.

When something is **Flavour Of The Month**, it is temporarily in fashion. The phrase is one of the most enduring advertising slogans of the last century and originates in the American ice cream parlours during the 1950s. To encourage customers to try different flavours and increase the sales of less popular types of ice cream, parlours would lower the price of a certain flavour for a month-long promotion. That month's cheap ice cream would be widely promoted as 'the flavour of the month'.

To **Get Someone's Goat** means to really irritate and annoy a person. This is an American phrase from the early part of the 20th century. Goats have long been considered to have a calming influence on horses and for this reason were often the stable mates of highly strung race horses, especially while being stabled at an unfamiliar race track. But sometimes a fancied stallion's chance of success would be torpedoed by shady opponents, who would slip into the stable and take the goat away. The result was an irritated and nervy racehorse who performed badly in the race.

To hear something **On The Grapevine** means to have obtained information through gossip and rumour while remaining unaware of the true source. William Morse invented the telegraph in America and first used it in a demonstration to Congress on 24 May 1844. Such was the enthusiasm for this new system of communication that companies all over America rushed to put up telegraph lines, often cutting many corners. In 1859 a Colonel Bee began work on a line between Virginia City, Nevada and Placerville, California and to save time and money decided to use trees instead of fixed telegraph poles. But the natural movement of trees soon pulled and stretched the line, leaving it coiled and tangled resembling one of the wild grapevines in California. From then on any general source of information was known in that area as 'the grapevine' and the term quickly spread throughout the land.

When something has **Gone Haywire** it is considered to be an uncontrollable rambling mess. The expression originated in the early 20th century in America with the introduction of a strong, thin metal wire, which was used to bind hay bales. Once snipped, the taut haywire would spring dangerously through the air and then be piled up in the corner of a yard in a tangled mass. Later farmers would use the rusting haywire to make temporary repairs to fences and tools and the overall chaotic mess with everything connected with the haywire resulted in the phrase being used to describe general untidy disorder.

Hobo is an American term for a travelling worker, rather than a 'tramp' (who travels without working) or a 'bum' who does neither. The origin of the phrase is the word 'hoe-boy', a **freelance** farm worker travelling with his tools (hoes) looking for work.

To **Hold The Fort** is to maintain normality and keep things running in the absence of others. During the American Civil War (1861–65), General Sherman immortalised the phrase during the battle of Allatoona in 1864. When gathering his army on top of Mount Kennesaw, near Atlanta, Georgia, Sherman signalled down to General Corse that reinforcements were arriving and he must 'hold the fort' until he had gathered enough men to mount an attack on the siege soldiers. The phrase made its way to Britain via the poet Philip Bliss (1838–76), who wrote about spiritual assistance in times of difficulty: 'Hold the fort for I am coming, Jesus signals still.' Popular American evangelists Moody and Sankey introduced the poem to the British public during their religious campaign in 1873.

Keeping Up With The Joneses is an expression for attempting to stay the financial and social equals of better-off friends or neighbours. Of American origin, the phrase began in a popular comic strip-cartoon of the same name by Arthur R. Momand. Beginning in 1913 *Keeping Up With The Joneses* ran for 28 years and was syndicated throughout US newspapers. Momand based the comedy around his own family's real-life attempt to maintain a show of material wealth on a limited income. Years later, in 1955, Momand wrote to CE Funk explaining his ideas. 'We had been living way beyond our means in our endeavour to keep up with the well-to-do class which lived around us in Cedarhurst. I also noticed most of our friends were doing the same: the $10,000 chap was trying to keep up with the $20,000-a-year man. I decided it would make good comic-strip material, so sat down and drew up six strips. At first I thought of calling it *Keeping Up With The Smiths*, but in the end decided "Jones" was more euphonious [pleasant sounding].'

A **Kangaroo Court** is an irregular (or illegal) tribunal that is conducted with complete disregard for due legal process. In America during the 19th century it was common for court procedure to miss out legal steps in order to obtain a popular or convenient conviction. This was known as jumping though the procedure of justice. It was first recorded in America in 1853 and has clear links with the Californian gold rush of 1849, which was joined by many Australian prospectors. During this time informal courts were set up to deal with so-called illegal prospectors who were known as claim jumpers. Many of these were Australian and it isn't difficult to see how the phrase passed over into wider use. It became a well-known phrase in Britain when applied to the dubious tribunals used by trade unions to deal with members who were regarded as strike-breakers.

To **Knock The Spots Off** means to beat easily, without too much effort. This phrase is of American origin and can be traced back to the mid-19th century when it was in common use. At carnivals and festivals all over America one of the most popular side shows was the shooting gallery, where cowboys, farmers and children would all pit their skills on the firing range. The most commonly used target, and the one in greatest supply, was a playing card and each sharpshooter would aim to remove as many of the 'spots' on the card as possible. The one who shot them all off would emerge as the winner.

The slang term for an Englishman in America is a **Limey**, which is sometimes used with affection and at other times disparagingly. In 1795 the Royal Navy began to issue fresh limes and other citrus fruits to the Fleet when it became known that their juice prevented a debilitating disease called scurvy, which was caused by a lack of Vitamin C, and many long distance sailors were affected by it. As a result Americans started calling British sailors 'Lime Juicers' or 'Limeys'.

On land, scurvy was known as the 'Spring Disease' as it usually occurred during these months when the body was lacking in vitamin C as a result of having few, if any, fresh vegetables and fruit to eat over the winter months. This is apparently also where the tradition of giving children oranges in their Christmas stockings originated, as an attempt to combat Spring Disease.

Lock, Stock And Barrel is a phrase used to indicate something in its entirety. This phrase has an American origin and can be traced to a US senator who persuaded the Senate to manufacture muskets in three parts: the lock, the stock and the barrel. This way the weapons could be easily transported in separate parts, preventing theft, and damaged guns could be rebuilt using spare parts from others. The idea was adopted and from that day onwards, soldiers found they needed the 'lock, stock and barrel' (everything) in order to make up a weapon.

To be **Mending Fences** is to be re-establishing working relationships with another person after a disagreement. *The Oxford Dictionary of Quotations* includes 'Good fences make good neighbours' as a common 17th-century proverb, but this is an American ranching expression dating back to the birth of the new country when land and boundary disputes were commonplace. Many settlers would argue over who was responsible for lost cattle and other livestock escaping through damaged fencing, but sensible landowners were soon out mending their fences together rather than arguing over the blame.

In 1879 an American senator made a homecoming speech in which he told the people of Mansfield, Ohio, 'I have come home to look after my fences.' It is not known if he meant that literally, or if he intended to rebuild personal or business relationships after his spell away in the Senate. But it is known that in October 1890 the *Daily Republican* of Mitchell County ran a headline, after much political fall-out during an electoral campaign, COMING TO MEND FENCES. The article confirmed 'an announcement that Consul General John C. New is on his way to this county. He has created quite a stir among Republican politicians, and there is a belief that he is coming to assume the personal direction of the campaign.'

A person **Throwing Mud Around** is generally bad mouthing and slandering somebody. The origin of this expression is nothing to do with the hapless Dr Mudd (see **Name Is Mud**), but a section of the American newspaper media in the early 1800s. Journalists who sullied other people's reputations were regarded as 'mud slingers' and their newspapers 'the mud press'. More recently it has become known as 'the gutter press'.

Your **Neck Of The Woods** is used to imply a person's neighbourhood. Way back in the early history of colonial America, the British began putting names to places in an attempt to give that new country some sense of its own identity. In doing so there was a deliberate attempt to avoid traditionally English-sounding names such as Dell, Fen, Moor, Heath and Ford. Instead words like Hollow, Fork, Stick and Foot were used. The only word that seems to have travelled is 'neck', which had been used in England since the mid-1500s to describe a narrow strip of land surrounded by water. But the settlers across the pond used the word to describe narrow strips of woodland in the new country and native Indian

228

settlements, often located in the forests, were identified by which 'neck of the woods' they could be found in.

When an event or situation **Pans Out Nicely** we are usually quite satisfied as things have gone in our favour. During the great Californian Gold Rush between 1848 and 1855, prospectors and miners carried a pan in their search for the precious metal. These pans were large sieves into which silt, mud and residue from a stream was shovelled and then washed through. Hopefully, large pieces of gold would remain in the pan after the earth had been rinsed out. If gold was found then things had panned out nicely; if not then they had not panned out very well at all.

To **Pass The Buck** is an easy thing to do, as it means avoiding your responsibility by passing it on to others. During the 19th century, the game of poker was one of the most popular pastimes in the mid-west of America. As part of the game, each player has to take a turn at dealing, which at times is worth avoiding as it means declaring the first stake (bet). Back in those Wild West days the most common knife was known as a buckhorn knife (so-called as the handle was carved from the horn of a buck). One of these knives would be placed in front of whoever was due to deal the next hand but if the stakes were running too high, he opted out of his turn by passing the buckhorn knife on to the next player. Even if he then chose to play the hand he still avoided the responsibility of setting the bets next time around by 'passing the buck'.

Later, at the great casinos and gaming houses in Las Vegas, a silver dollar was used in place of a knife and that is how the slang term 'buck' for the US dollar arose.

The first recorded use of 'passing the buck' was by Mark Twain in 1872 but the expression was known by 1865. Later, in 1945, President Truman famously had a plaque made and placed on his desk in the Oval Office of the White House. It read 'The Buck Stops Here', an obvious declaration that he was prepared to accept responsibility for all the decisions taken during his term of office. Presidents Carter, Ford and Nixon all copied the idea.

Riding Shotgun is the phrase often used to describe the person sitting next to a driver. A shotgun is a long, smoothbore twin-barrelled weapon that fires a scatter load rather than a single bullet and was sometimes known as a scattergun or a two-shot gun. First invented in 1776, it was regularly used during the days of stagecoach travel, particularly in the Wild West of America. Because of the wide range of the shot, it was especially useful in remote areas when stagecoach drivers and postal express messengers might be confronted by outlaws or wild animals such as bears or a pack of wolves. The shotgun could be fired generally in the right direction and was likely to hit something and scare others in the group away. By the turn of the 19th century all stagecoaches had a shotgun guard riding next to the driver keeping a look out for danger and postal messengers even became known as 'shotgun messengers'.

In 1891 the *Stevens Point Journal* published an article describing shotgun guards: 'Of all the devices and inventions for the protection of treasure and circumvention of the road agent, the only one that has stood the test of time and experience is a big, ugly-tempered man with a sawed-off shotgun on the box. It is the business of a man with a sawed-off shotgun not to let the outlaw get the drop, but to blaze away as soon as he shows up. The gun is sawed off for the greater convenience of the messenger in potting road agents. It is loaded with buckshot and scatters like a charge of bribery fired into a California legislature.'

Wells Fargo & Co express messengers always had a man riding shotgun for the driver and outlaws came to realise that if a Wells Fargo driver had no shotgun passenger then his stagecoach carried nothing of value. The practice of having shotgun riders continued with the development of the rail networks across America and the expression passed over into wider public use thanks to the classic John Wayne film *Stagecoach*, produced in 1939. In 1921 the *Washington Post's* magazine of fiction published a popular story called *The Fighting Fool* that began with the sentence: 'Lum Martin,' shouted McMonagle, owner of the Cow Ranch saloon who was waving his finger in front of Benson's face. 'That's the man – Lum Martin. He's ridin' shotgun for Wells Fargo, or was until last week, and he's over in my saloon right now, playin' solitaire.'

Finally, the great Spaghetti Western films, popular in both Britain and America during the 1950s and 1960s, so named because they were produced by Italian-owned film studios, ensured that the expression is here to stay.

The phrase **Shotgun Wedding** also arose during the same period to describe a forced marriage. Outlaws or ranchers who had made a young girl pregnant would be encouraged to marry her at the point of a shotgun by the girl's father and brothers.

To **Rope Somebody In** means to involve a person in a project or event against their wishes or judgement. It is an early American ranching expression and thinking about how cowboys lassoo horses on the plains to bring them into the paddocks it is easy to see how it became part of our language.

To be **Sold Down The River** means to have been misled and that a promise or other assurances have not been met. It is an American phrase by origin and relates to slavery in the 1800s. Wealthy landowners would hand pick the slaves they regarded suitable to live on the estates with their families in relative comfort. Some were even promised such a lifestyle as they left Africa, India and the East Indies in search of a better future. The reality, however, was that those regarded unsuitable to live with the families were put on a boat and sent down the Mississippi river where they were sold to the plantations as slave labour. There the living conditions were appalling and the wretched folk had been well and truly 'sold down the river' by the land of opportunity.

A **Straw Poll** is an expression used to describe a study of general opinion. It is widely used in politics to assess the overall views of the people by taking small random samples of opinion and using that to measure wider feeling. The use of the phrase began in America in 1824 when reporters from the *Harrisburg Pennsylvanian* questioned a sample of voters in Wilmington in an attempt to predict the overall result. Their findings proved accurate and were considered such a success that the idea caught on and has been used in almost every election ever since. The actual wording comes from the practice of throwing a handful of straw into the air to determine the direction of the wind.

Taking A Rain Check is a term used when declining an invitation on one occasion, but keeping it open for another day. The phrase began during the 19th century when American baseball clubs noticed dwindling crowd levels during the winter months. It became obvious that fair-weather fans were not interested in games played on cold or wet days, especially if there was any chance of bad weather stopping play. That was until one bright marketing spark came up with the idea of promising a 'rain check' (or rain ticket) to any fan who wanted to leave, up to a certain point during a match, because of bad weather. The 'rain check' became a safety net for fans as it would entitle them to attend a game on another day if the one they paid for was washed out, ensuring their entry fee had not been wasted. The best part for the club was that they not only kept the money, but also guaranteed the fan would return again another day *and* they retained his goodwill for the future. The practice spread and it later became common for American baseball fans to 'take a rain check' halfway through dull and boring games, whatever the weather.

Talking Turkey means to have frank and direct discussions, which can be blunt in their delivery. Turkeys were first found in America among the native Indians. At first European settlers confused the bird with the guinea fowls (natives of Africa) they had in their home countries. Thinking the bird was from Turkey, they developed a taste for it and soon the gobbler was in high demand at the settlements and reservations. As a result all serious discussions with the native Indians soon became known as 'talking about turkey' and the phrase became part of the English language in America, before crossing the water to Britain. *Brewer's Dictionary* offers a second suggested origin of the practice of turkey hunters attracting their prey by imitating its gobbling noises ('talking turkey'). Apparently the birds would then return the call and reveal their whereabouts for the hunter. Take your pick.

There Is More Than One Way To Skin A Cat is a common saying to indicate there are several ways in achieving a particular goal. Cat lovers will be relieved to know this has nothing to do with their feline friends. Instead it relates to catfish – long a popular source of food and easy to snare, but the skin is difficult to remove. I am reliably informed there are several ways to skin a catfish successfully, the best being to drop the fish into boiling water, which allows the skin to be easily peeled away from the meat.

There Is No Such Thing As A Free Lunch means that nothing actually comes for free and, even when it seems to, there is usually a hidden cost. In the 1840s American bars and restaurants began attracting customers by offering a free lunch to anyone buying a drink. But these lunches were usually only salty snacks that, once eaten, would encourage the customer to drink more and quench his subsequent thirst. It was soon noted these drinkers were spending more than they originally intended and didn't even benefit from a proper lunch. Such tactics still work and are the reason why so many modern pubs and bars can be found offering free bowls of salted crisps and peanuts to drinkers. John Farmer, in his book *Americanisms*, published in 1899, noted: 'The free lunch fiend is one who makes a meal of what is really provided as a snack, but shamefacedly manages to get something more than his money's worth.'

To put in your **Two-Penny's Worth** means to add an opinion, which could be regarded as almost worthless. The origin of this phrase is found in America when the US Treasury issued a two-cent coin in 1864, along with three- and 20-cent coins. They were the first US coins bearing the phrase 'In God We Trust'. The two-cent coin, being the lowest in value, was soon used as a self-deprecating and modest way of offering an opinion and by the late 19th century 'let me have my two cents' worth' was a standard preamble to offering suggestions. This was done because if an opinion was later regarded as worthless a person could claim they had warned in advance it may have had a low value. The phrase crossed the Atlantic in the early 20th century and has been in use in Britain ever since.

To be **On The Wagon** means a person is no longer drinking alcohol. In the US water carts and wagons began carrying drinking water, or water for cleaning the streets, in 1900. At that time, a person who was known to have given up alcohol could often be found waiting for the water wagon to arrive so they could quench their thirst. People would flock around as the wagon arrived and reformed heavy drinkers were said to actually ride on the wagon around town so they could take on as much water as possible and help quash the craving for alcohol. Many Americans, including criminals who had blamed drink for their crimes, were encouraged to sign a pledge that they were 'on the water wagon', which meant they would rather drink water from the wagon than the demon whisky. The expression became widely used in America throughout the 20th century.

To be **From The Wrong Side Of The Tracks** is to have come from a poor and underprivileged area of town. In days gone by this alone would deem you socially inferior to those born to better conditions.

This is an American expression from the days when great towns and cities grew up along the newly laid railroads. In such towns the better off would live upwind of the station so the prevailing smog, fumes, smells and sounds would be blown away from their houses. The less fortunate, such as the actual workers, would be housed downwind in less desirable circumstances.

This practice, if not the phrase, originated in England where the poorer districts of many cities are in the eastern areas, determined by the prevailing west or southwesterly winds. It first began during the great trading days when the docks were the busiest and smelliest part of any major town and the westerly winds would ensure those living to the west of the docks lived in the most desirable areas.

239

14: FOOD AND DRINK

Barmy Army is a phrase used to describe a rowdy group of people, usually sports fans who are excitable, volatile and often drunk. 'Barm' is the froth produced by fermenting alcohol and in English prisons inmates used to feign madness by 'putting on the barmy stick' (frothing at the mouth). In 1912 Fred Murray wrote and published a popular song which includes the lines 'Ginger you're barmy, why don't you join the army.' This formed part of a popular limerick during the First World War when the lines 'you'll get knocked out by a bottle of stout, Ginger you're barmy' were added. In 1994 rowdy English cricket fans, who had followed the national team to Australia for the Ashes tour, were affectionately nicknamed the

'Barmy Army', an obvious equivalent of Scotland's Tartan Army of football fans.

When somebody **Brings Home The Bacon** they have achieved something notable, or won a prize or award. There are two possible explanations for this phrase. The first is an ancient game, popular at country fairs up and down the land. Men would chase a heavily greased pig around a ring and whoever finally caught and held on to the pig was given it as a prize to take home. Such winners were said to have 'taken home the bacon'. The second, and far more likely, explanation originates from a tradition known as the Dunmow Flitch Trials. Established by a noblewoman called Juga in 1104, at Great Dunmow in Essex, the trial was a challenge to all married couples in England to live for a year and a day in complete harmony, without so much as a cross word between them. The prize offered was a flitch of bacon (a whole side) but in over 500 years there were only eight winners. The tradition was re-established in 1855 and these days are held every four years, often with celebrities taking part. Claimants of the flitch are required to stand in front of a jury of 12 (six maidens and six bachelors of Great Dunmow) and prove their worthiness during a day-long family event. The winners 'take home the bacon'. These days, it would seem, the noblewoman's bacon is safe.

As Drunk As A Lord is used to describe anyone in an advanced state of intoxication. During the 18th and 19th centuries heavy drinking was popular among the nobility and men of fashion prided themselves on their talent to consume vast amounts of wine. As lords and noblemen rarely worked, they would indulge themselves throughout the day and by the time a hunting party retired to nearby hostelries in the evening they would often be rolling drunk. Villagers and farm workers could rarely afford such behaviour, but when one of them did they were described as 'drunk as a lord'.

Eating Humble Pie is used to indicate somebody who has to admit to being wrong in public, perhaps in humiliating fashion, and is looked down upon by those once considered equal. This hierarchy was established during the medieval hunts and the subsequent banquets. During the feast the lord of the manor, and his peers, would be served the finest cuts of venison. But the

243

entrails and offal, known at the time as 'umbles', would be baked into a pie and served to those of a lower standing or out of favour. It was common practice for people to be humiliated by finding themselves sat at the wrong end of the table and served 'umble pie'.

In *David Copperfield*, the Charles Dickens novel published in 1850, one of the characters, Uriah Heep, said, 'I got to know what umbleness did and I took to it. I ate umble pie with an appetite.' That's how the phrase was popularised in Britain.

Gone For A Burton is a phrase used to indicate that somebody has had an unfortunate mishap, or that something or someone has been lost altogether. Before the Second World War, Burton's Ales ran an advert depicting a football team with one player missing from the line-up, leaving a gap in the team photograph. The caption explained that the player had 'Gone for a Burton'. This slogan was picked up by the RAF during the war and used as slang for a missing pilot who had crashed in action into the sea (aka the drink) and was affectionately referred to as having 'gone for a Burton'. He would be missing from photographs in future.

Gone To Pot is widely used to describe something that is no longer of any real use, or a person not in the fit condition they used to be in. A reference dating back to the 16th century show that cuts of meat which, in those pre-refrigerated days, were on the verge of hardening and no longer edible, would be chopped into small pieces and cooked up in a stew-pot. Therefore meat beyond its best would be described as having 'gone to the pot'.

The phrase **Hair Of The Dog** is a shortened version of 'the hair of the dog that bit you'. Early English medical theory suggested rubbing the hair of a particular dog into the wound of its bite would cure the ill effects and heal the wound. The phrase was used in many variations until settling down as a hangover remedy. These days a few more drinks the day after a major session is said to cure the effects of a hangover and is known as 'the hair of the dog'.

245

To be **One Over The Eight** is a phrase used to describe the inebriated on the basis that it was generally assumed a man could drink eight pints of beer (one gallon) before he became too drunk to function. Fraser and Gibbon's **Soldier and Sailor Words** of 1925 contains the phrase: 'One over the eight is one drink too many. Slightly intoxicated, the presumption being that an average "moderate" man can safely drink eight glasses of beer.' Sounds about right to me.

To **Open A Can Of Worms** is to reveal, perhaps unexpectedly, a whole new set of problems that prove to be complicated and possibly scandalous. Once tinned and preserved food had been introduced in the early 1800s, it became regular fixture in homes across Britain, so people would be disgusted if they opened a can only to find it seething with maggots and worms. This was obviously well before sell-by dates had been introduced and made part of the law.

In 1795 Napoleon Bonaparte, who famously declared that an army 'marches on its stomach', offered a reward of 12,000 francs to anybody who could devise a method of preserving food for his army. However it was an Englishman, Peter

Durand, who received the first patent from King George III for a tin-plated iron can as a food container in 1810 (five years before Napoleon met his Waterloo). Strangely enough, it would be another 48 years before the can opener was invented.

When we **Propose A Toast** we are raising a glass to drink in somebody's honour. During the 15th and 16th centuries a small piece of spiced toast would be added to a glass of wine in society households to improve the flavour and filter the sediment. This was known as 'toasted wine' or 'toasting wine' and when it was drunk in honour of another person, usually a lady, the phrase 'to drink a toasted wine' was used. It was in common use in Britain by 1700.

15: HUNTING

To **Beat Around The Bush** is to approach a subject indirectly without tackling the central point directly. The saying is a 300-year-old hunting phrase relating to beaters, who use sticks against a bush or undergrowth (wherever game has taken refuge) with the intention of scaring it out and into the line of the hunters' guns. That is known as catching a quarry by 'beating around the bush'.

When something or someone is **Clapped Out**, it is worn out, exhausted and unable to continue. For the origin of this phrase we delve into the sport of hare coursing, a centuries-old custom and the forerunner of today's greyhound racing. While greyhound racing is relatively civilised, its predecessor was barbaric and cruel. In the name of fun a pair of greyhounds would be set after a hare in a race to catch it. Often, in the countryside, the chase would take quite some time and the hare, in a bid to catch its breath, would find a chance to stop and sit up on its haunches. Its fear and exhaustion was so great, and its breathing so heavy, that the hare's chest heaved in and out, forcing the front legs to move backwards and forwards in time, giving the appearance of clapping. This is what led to the phrase 'clapped out' entering the English language.

Fair Game is used to describe somebody, or something, that may be legitimately pursued and assaulted. In the 1700s King George III introduced 32 new hunting laws in a bid to reduce poaching and protect landowners, such as himself, from theft of livestock. The idea was to keep hunting the privilege of the aristocracy, but was cloaked in the notion that without controls game stock would be severely depleted. By the beginning of the following century it was illegal for anyone to remove game from any land apart from the squire and his eldest son. Anybody taking even a single pheasant could be transported to Australia for seven years. But some small animals and birds, mainly vermin, were not included in the legislation and these were listed in the regulations as 'fair game'.

The Game Is Up is used to suggest a secret scheme or a plot has been revealed. It is often thought to relate to a sporting event that has come to an end, but in fact its origin lies in hunting. Those hunting game on country estates employ beaters who drive pheasants and other game birds out into the open (see **Beating Around The Bush**). The shout 'the game is up' suggests the bird's hiding place has been found and they have been driven up into the path of the guns. The shoot can begin.

To take something **Hook, Line And Sinker** means to be gullible enough to believe a dubious tale in its entirety. A hungry and gullible fish will not only swallow a baited hook but also the lead weight (a sinker) and some of the line.

Taking **Pot Luck** means to take whatever is randomly given. This expression was widely used in the Middle Ages when a cooking pot containing a range of ingredients, such as a stew, was always on the fire. Any visitor being offered a meal would be ladled out whatever was in the pot and they called that 'pot luck'. This is also the origin of the phrase **Pot Shot**, which meant the hunter would shoot at any animal he saw, rather than track a particular game, to go in the family cooking pot.

Red Herring is used to describe something that provides a false or misleading clue, often in a detective story. In the 18th and 19th centuries herring was one of the most widely caught fish in the seas around Britain. In those pre-refrigerated days it would be preserved by salting and smoking. This smoking process would turn the herring a deep brownish red colour. Heavily smoked herring would also have a particularly strong and pungent smell. For the origins of the phrase we turn to hunting in the early 1800s and hunt saboteurs. It's true: there must have been an early version of the modern fox lover as on hunt days the strong-smelling fish would be dragged along the hunt route and away from the foxes. This confused the hounds, which followed the scent of the 'red herring' rather than that of the fox. So effective was this tactic that the phrase passed into common English usage.

A **Stalking Horse** is a name given to someone who is put forward to mask another's ambitions and mislead an opponent. Stalking horses rarely benefit from their own actions; instead they agree to act in order to gauge support for a challenge to an incumbent leader. The phrase stems from an old English hunting practice, dating back to 1519, whereby a huntsman would walk behind a specially trained horse and reach his target without alarming it, as he would have done if he went towards it unhidden and on foot. Once within range the hunter could bag the unsuspecting game with relative ease.

16: SIMPLE PHRASES, SIMPLE ORIGINS

When something is **Above Board** it implies everything has been carried out honestly and in the proper way, and there is no need for suspicion. This is a gaming term and relates to the practice of a player keeping his hands above the gaming board at all times, where the other players could see them. This way nobody could be accused of cheating. Even a player simply scratching his knee could lead to suggestions the game had not been played fully 'above the board'.

Alive And Kicking is used to suggest someone or something is lively and active. In the last century the origin was thought to relate to a market fishmonger who used the phrase to indicate his fish were so fresh they were still 'kicking' in the trays. But there is an earlier theory which will have us believe the phrase was in use during the Middle Ages when, during pregnancy, expectant mothers would describe their unborn as 'alive and kicking' in the womb.

All In The Same Boat is an expression used to illustrate a group of people all facing exactly the same benefit, or adverse affect, of a particular event. The phrase has a nautical origin and alludes to sailors in high seas all facing exactly the same peril should the ship go down, regardless of whether they were the captain or a lowly deck hand. Everybody faced the same risk.

As Bright As A Button is used to describe somebody who is mentally alert and quick-witted. The expression dates back to early military uniforms that had metal buttons, which needed to be kept polished and sparkling.

The expression **Back To The Drawing Board** is one we might use when our best intentions and well made plans fail to work. It means we have to try a new idea. This phrase became popular during the Second World War when the *New Yorker* magazine published a cartoon depicting a newly built aircraft exploding into thousands of pieces before it had even taken off. The designer, apparently unperturbed, simply shrugged his shoulders and remarked, 'Oh well, so it is back to the drawing board again.'

To **Bank On Someone** means to rely upon or completely trust a person. Prior to the modern bank many people kept whatever wealth they had either about their person or hidden away in as safe a place as possible. In medieval Venice, once the centre of world trade, men set up benches or counters in the main squares and would trade the various world currencies that passed around the city. These men were universally trusted and relied upon and traders could borrow, exchange and even leave money with them while they returned to their native countries. The bench men would then trade that currency with other travellers and traders would often collect even larger sums than they left behind the next time they returned to Venice. The system was an early form of world banking and the Venetians were regarded as people who could be 'banked upon' (or with). The Italian word for bench or counter is 'banco'.

To **Barge In** on something is to intrude or abruptly interrupt a situation. Since the 17th century development of the English waterways, which linked most major towns and cities, the boats used have been flat-bottomed barges. Due to the cumbersome handling of these vessels, collisions were common and by the late 1800s schoolboys used the term for bumping into or 'hustling' somebody. By the turn of the century the phrase had entered the common English language meaning to interrupt without invitation, sometimes with physical force.

If you are dressed in your **Best Bib And Tucker** you are wearing your finest outfit, your Sunday best. In the 17th century it was common for all society men to wear fashionable bibs to protect their morning and dinner suits from spills. The women wore lace or muslin, which was tucked into the top of low cut dresses (to protect their modesty) and known as tuckers. Couples dressed in their finest for special occasions were known to have gone out in their 'best bib and tuckers'. The phrase is now applied to either sex in their best clothes.

A **Bigwig** is a slang term for somebody in authority. In 17th-century England the fashion was for gentlemen to wear wigs, a tradition that lasts to this day in areas such as the law courts and the House of Lords. Back then gentlemen's wigs were not only fashionable but also indicated social status – the aristocracy, bishops and High Court judges were all afforded full-length wigs which represented their position at the top of society. This level or class became known as the 'bigwigs'. The tradition is fading these days as many High Court judges opt not to wear the traditional head-dress, believing it makes the judiciary look remote and out of touch.

To **Bite Off More Than You Can Chew** is an expression we use to indicate someone has taken on more than they can manage, perhaps greedily. This is an American phrase traceable to the 1800s and the popular habit of chewing tobacco. Such tobacco was produced in lengths and it was as common to offer others a 'bite' as it is these days to offer somebody a cigarette from a packet. The greedy would take such a large bite they were unable to chew it properly but tried instead to break it down and save some for later, without their benefactor realising it. Naturally people became wise to this, hence the admonition 'don't bite off more than you can chew'.

To be in the **Black Books** is to be out of favour and disgraced. Originally a black book held the names of those who were to be punished. Henry VIII, during his battle against the Pope in the 16th century, compiled a black book listing monasteries he regarded as promoters of 'manifest sin, vicious, carnal and abominable living'. Using the Black Book as evidence, the King was able to persuade Parliament to dissolve the monasteries and assign their wealth to the Crown. Given that burning at the stake and public disembowelment were among Henry's favourite methods of persuasion, it paid not to be in his Black Book, and it was Henry's purges that give rise to the idiom we use. Later in the century merchants used black books to make lists of people who failed to pay for goods and of those who had been made bankrupt. In 1726, *The Secret History Of The University Of Oxford* records that the Proctor had a 'black book' and that 'no person whose name was listed may proceed to a degree'.

A **Black Leg** is a person who continues to work when his colleagues are out on strike. Originally a northern mining term which evolved from working miners being identifiable by their black boots and coal-covered black trousers. To see a 'black leg' walking past during a strike meant you saw a strike-breaker.

A **Blacklist** is a list naming those who have broken laws or other agreements and codes. This is closely associated to Henry's **Black Book** but as a list, once compiled, names were neither added nor removed as they might be in a running book. The first Blacklist was compiled during the 1660s after Charles II was crowned King. One of the first things the Restoration Parliament did was to have a list of names drawn up of all those held responsible for the trial and execution of his father, Charles I, in 1649. Those on the list were ruthlessly hunted down and publicly executed in an act of revenge. The new King, however, was opposed to the bloodshed and fought, unsuccessfully, for clemency. In the end only nine of the original 60 names on the blacklist, were publicly slaughtered.

To have a **Bone To Pick** with someone suggests some sorting out until all the facts of a particular dispute are apparent to all parties. The phrase stems from the 16th century and relates to a dog biting and chewing on a butcher's bone until it was picked clean. A **Bone Of Contention** suggests an argument or a fight and also originates in the 16th century relating to two dogs fighting over a bone.

A person who **Wouldn't Say Boo To A Goose** is usually timid and apprehensive. Throughout medieval Britain geese were a staple part of nearly every diet and in plentiful supply. Geese would litter the village streets and would sometimes make a nuisance of themselves. But they are also known to be very shy and timid animals and easy to scare away. The earliest printed example of the expression was in 1572 and describes a person who 'would not say shoo to a goose'.

To **Buttonhole** a person is to detain and talk to somebody who may have previously been avoiding the conversation. The phrase is a reference to the practice, dating back to the 18th century, of gentlemen discreetly slipping a finger into the buttonhole of another's morning suit, ensuring they stay and listen to what they have to say. A variation of this was to hold on to the suit's buttons (button-hold). Either way it was a tactful manner of restraining somebody for a quiet word.

When something is or has been **On The Cards** it means it was predictable and very likely to happen. This is a simple phrase with a simple origin. In the late 18th century, fortune-tellers were a very popular part of society and tarot cards were regularly used to predict a person's future. When a predictable event took place it was common to conclude that it had previously been 'on the cards'.

To be **Carpeted** is to be reprimanded in a severe way by a superior. The saying can be traced to the days of the Victorian civil service where status was of utmost importance and to attain a level which afforded a civil servant an office with a carpet was success indeed. To be reprimanded in such a way as a person was moved back to an office with wooden floorboards was considered serious and shameful. Status-conscious Victorians would want to avoid a 'carpeting' at all costs. How did they ever create that Empire?

Off The Cuff means speaking without notes or carrying out a task with no real preparation. In Victorian times men wore shirts with stiff, detachable collars and cuffs, making them easier to keep clean. In order to give the impression they were speaking to an audience from the heart politicians and after-dinner speakers wanted to address gatherings without any visible script or notes. They would, however, write key notes about topics they would like to cover on their cuffs which they could refer to from time to time. They might also make additional notes during the speech of a fellow politician so they would be reminded to counter any points made by their opponents. This all gave the impression the speaker was fully prepared and articulate enough not to need a script but in fact they had notes all the time, written out 'on the cuffs'.

As Dead As A Dodo means long obsolete, finished and no longer available. A dodo was a large flightless bird that can thank the Portuguese for its name. Being flightless, because its wings were too small for its fat body, the dodo would be taken on board a ship at harbour and, unable to escape, kept alive as fresh meat to be eaten by hungry sailors as required. When the Portuguese found them on the island of Mauritius they named them 'doudo', meaning stupid in their language. By the end of the 17th century they had been eaten into extinction (becoming one of the first recorded species to do so) and the expression passed over into the English language.

A **Dead Ringer** is somebody who looks just like another. In medieval Britain the medical profession was not quite as refined as it is now, and often anybody found not to show signs of life was regarded as dead, when they might have been simply unconscious. (This was also before comas were fully understood.) It was not uncommon for bodies to be exhumed later and corpses found with their fingers worn to the bone, an obvious indication somebody had returned to consciousness and tried to claw their way out of a coffin. So horrific was this image that the English gentry began mistrusting medical opinions and buried their loved ones with string attached to their wrists, connected to a bell above the grave. Anybody who returned to consciousness and found themselves prematurely buried could attract attention by ringing the bell and it has been recorded this actually worked. Many 'bodies' were exhumed after bells were rung and some people carried on with their normal lives. But when spotted in the street startled acquaintances would cry to each other, 'That looks just like Jack Jones – I thought he was dead' to which they would receive the reply, 'Yes, he must be a dead ringer.' And that, believe it or not, is true.

266

Somebody who has **Gone To The Dogs** is thought to be down on his luck and whose appearance and behaviour has deteriorated. At the great medieval dining tables scraps and partially eaten food was usually thrown out for the dogs. Often beggars and the starving could be found rooting around with the dogs trying to find something to eat.

To **Earmark** something is to intend to set something aside as your own. The origin of this saying is found in the ancient art of marking cattle ears with a ring or a tab. Owners, or potential owners at market, would set cattle aside in this way, indicating an intention to buy. Centuries prior to that this practice even included human property: slaves would have 'their ears borne through with an awl' to identify ownership. This practice is also the root of the later fashion of wearing earrings. In relatively recent years the term spread to the wider use it has today.

Eavesdroppers are people who deliberately try to overhear another's conversation without detection. Centuries ago houses in England had no gutters and drain pipes. Instead the roofs extended far past the walls of the house enabling rainwater to drip to the ground away from the building. The area between the dripping rain and the walls was originally known as the 'eavesdrip' and latterly the 'eavesdrop'. The eavesdrop also served as a shelter for passing pedestrians who would stand close to the walls of a building and out of the rain, but they could also overhear conversations going on inside a house, and became known as 'eavesdroppers'.

At The End Of My Tether means I am at the very limit of my patience and self-control. In the Middle Ages a grazing animal would often be tethered to a post, ensuring it didn't stray beyond a certain small area. But, once the animal arrived at the limit of its tether, unable to quite reach pastures new, it would become frustrated, irritable and sometimes traumatised to the point of despair. Sound familiar?

NNNGG!

To **Fly In The Face** of something means to do the opposite of what is usually expected, and often at some risk. This phrase has been in use for centuries and relates to hens who, when attacked by foxes, fly around their faces in an attempt to confuse and distract the wily old predator. Risky business indeed.

Freelance workers – often self-employed writers, journalists or musicians – are not continuously employed by a single organisation. In the Middle Ages when knights and lords fought for supremacy (and land), a freelancer was exactly that, a lance soldier for hire. The word used these days is mercenary but once upon a time a 'free lance' was exactly how it sounded. The phrase passed into modern English language as late as 1820 when Sir Walter Scott wrote in his novel *Ivanhoe*: 'Ivanhoe offers Richard the services of my Free Lancers.'

Having a **Frog In The Throat** suggests a person is unable to speak easily and clearly. There was a time, prior to clean drinking water being freely available, that folk would drink water drawn from ponds and streams. Medieval legend will have us believe that people feared swallowing frogspawn lest tadpoles would hatch in the stomach. The idea of a live frog trying to make an escape by way of the throat isn't a pleasant one (although

with garlic and a little white wine sauce it doesn't
seem too bad to the French).

To be **Up A Gum Tree** is to be caught in a
predicament from which there is no easy way out.
Eucalyptus trees are a characteristic of the
Australian continent, where many of them are also
known as gum trees. These species release copious
amounts of sap through the bark and while many
indigenous animals, such as the koala and possum,
have adapted to this condition, others haven't.
Some animals taking refuge up a gum tree can
therefore become trapped and at the mercy of
their prey.

To **Let Your Hair Down** usually means a
celebration or period of relaxation after a busy
time. Throughout history, working women have
pinned their hair up or perhaps worn a bonnet. At
the end of the day it was normal for long hair to
be let down again for washing or brushing and it
became a common expression to describe a lady
perhaps finishing a shift in a factory or mill.

The Old French word for uncovering or
revealing hair was dechevele, based on the Latin
word for hair, which is cheve. This, in turn, is how

the English word 'dishevel' evolved. An early reference can be found in *The English Treasury of Wit and Language*, published in 1655 by John Cotgrave: 'Descheveler, to discheuell; meaning to pull the haire around the eares.'

To **Haul Somebody Over The Coals** means to give them a severe tongue-lashing, and perhaps find out the truth of a matter. In the 15th century, heresy (practising unorthodox religions) was regarded as a crime against the Church and the punishment was death. The problem was that the crime of heresy was almost impossible to prove as few ever confessed to adopting their own religious opinions, so the powers that be came up with an ingenious method of deciding. Anybody accused of heresy would be tied and dragged over a burning bed of charcoal. If they died it was accepted the person was a heretic and deserved such a fate. However, if they lived they were freed, as it was thought God had protected the accused. So, while the supposed heretics died, the innocents were merely roasted. Brilliant!

When we **Break The Ice** we are taking the initiative in breaking down a formality and getting started on a project. This idiom is more than 500 years old and is common in many European languages. Years ago many major European rivers would ice over at the bank sides during the cold and bitter winters. The River Thames used to freeze completely and carnivals and fairs were held on the surface. But those relying on the rivers for their livelihood didn't enjoy those times quite so much and every morning, before they could set about their business, they would have to break the ice around the boats and cut a path out to where the water still flowed. For them 'breaking the ice' meant getting started on their day's work.

Ill-gotten Gains is a term for money, or other reward, obtained by dishonest means. The phrase we use today has been shortened from its original form: 'Ill-gotten gains never prosper.' The phrase first appeared in the early 16th century and was applied to the pirates of the English coastline and their booty. In 1592 William Shakespeare popularised the phrase in his play *Henry VI Part 3* when he included the line 'Didst thou never hear that things ill got had ever bad success?'

A **Kiss And Tell Story** is usually the details of the sex life of somebody who is well known told by a person nobody has ever heard of – until then (see also **Fifteen Minutes of Fame**). The phrase Kiss and *Sell* might be more accurate. Although regarded as a modern tabloid expression, it can be traced to the early 1700s and a farce written by the American author Gabriel Odingsell called *The Capricious Lovers*, first staged in 1726. In it, Odingsell had his characters acting the following scene:

> Mrs Mince-mode: Well, I don't know anything that would oblige me to quit the Country, so soon as this detested Custom of kissing and slabbering.

> Squire Pert: If you begin to grow angry. Smack's the Word again.

> Mrs Mince-mode: I tell you once for all I nauseate your Smacks, your rude, noisy Smacks.

> Graciana: I confess, Coz, there you have reason, for 'tis like kiss and tell.

273

A **Knee-Jerk Reaction** is an automatic and instant response to something, often without proper consideration and usually turns out to be foolish. Sir Michael Foster made the first written record of this expression in his medical textbook entitled Physiology, published in 1877. In explaining reflexes he writes: 'Striking the tendon directly below the patella [kneecap] gives rise to a sudden extension of the leg, known as the knee-jerk.' Hence, a knee-jerk reaction is an instant, often involuntary, response to a given situation.

When something is **Near The Knuckle** (usually a comment or remark) it is regarded as on the limit, as far as one should go. When carving a joint of meat a butcher will cut the flesh right down to the knuckle bone which would be the limit of the cut, therefore a remark near the knuckle is on the limit. The expression **Close To The Bone** means exactly the same thing.

A person who is **Long In The Tooth** is considered to be old and wise. There is no real proof as to whether the origin of this phrase comes from humans or animals, particularly horses. Our equine friends do not benefit from dental hygiene and therefore as they age their gums recede, leaving the teeth appearing longer in the mouth (see **Don't Look A Gift Horse In The Mouth**). However, our forefathers didn't have the benefits of modern dentistry either, so our elderly ancestors were affectionately regarded as being 'long in the tooth'.

The **Minutes Of A Meeting** are the notes taken as a record of what has been discussed and later circulated around participants as a reminder. Although this phrase has nothing to do with the minutes of an hour, it does come from the same Latin word minutus. Centuries ago, meeting notes were brief and written in very small handwriting for speed, and then later rewritten before being passed around the attendees. But the minutes were pronounced 'my newts' (as in very small) and the word was used to describe the short notes taken.

To be described as having **No Flies On You** means you are quick-witted, alert and active. The expression can be traced to the cattle ranches of both America and Australia and is first recorded during the mid-1800s. Quite simply the lively, active cattle and horses attracted few flies that preferred instead to settle on the slow, sluggish animals who would stay still for the longest period of time. The phrase became widely used very quickly and in the early 1900s even the Salvation Army put it to general use by adopting a hymn entitled 'There are no flies on Jesus'. It even included the classic observation 'There may be flies on me and you / but there are no flies on Jesus.'

A **Pecking Order** is a system of hierarchy controlling relationships on a social scale. This is a farming expression and reveals the strict chain of command in any hen coop. There is one powerful hen in every coop that has the right to peck any other hen without fear of reprisal. All other hens have a place below her and they instinctively know they can peck a hen below themselves in status, but never one above them. Ultimately there is one poor runt hen that is pecked by all of the others, but can only peck at grain. Parallel patterns appear all over human and animal society as groups naturally divide themselves in a social order.

To **Pigeon Hole** a person is to classify them and give them a specific identity when more than one might be more appropriate. The English used to keep pigeons as domestic birds, although not as pets, but for food. Pigeons generally do not stray too far from a place they are being fed, so folk would set small openings into walls, or build boxes with recesses that pigeons would naturally make their home, without realising they would later be eaten. These were known as pigeonholes. During the 18th century offices would have small compartments built into the furniture to file documents and, owing to the resemblance, these also became known as pigeonholes. These pigeonholes would each have categories and the documents in them would all have a similar theme, decided by the filing clerk. When a document had more than one reference it was up to the clerk to decide where it was to be placed and hence a document was 'pigeonholed'. But not always correctly.

Pipe Dreams are ideas and ambitions we have that are usually way above our levels of ability: something we can dream about but realistically have no chance of ever achieving. The expression emerged from the Victorian opium houses at a time when opiates were still legally used in Britain.

Opium was smoked in pipes and was well known for stirring up fanciful ideas and fantasies.

A **Pitched Battle** is a general free for all between warring factions. In days gone by, skirmishes would break out at random places where rivals chanced upon each other by accident. However, there would also be occasions when opponents would make arrangements for a 'pitch' to be agreed on in advance of a battle when there was something of importance that needed to be settled. As there would be no element of surprise, an army could prepare by increasing both their numbers and their weapons, so these 'pitched' battles would be the most aggressive and brutal of them all.

Related to this are the expressions **To Pitch In** to somebody, meaning to attack them verbally or physically and **To Pitch Up**, meaning to turn up at a place, usually without warning and perhaps seeking confrontation.

If you are asked to do something **Post Haste** you are being asked to do it quickly, without delay. When, during the 16th century, the English postal system began to develop around the country, it relied on horseback messengers. Because of the nature of the work, horses needed to be rested every 20–30 miles. This led to the emergence of posthouses all over the country which all provided fresh horses for messengers to use on longer journeys. The royal post was regarded as a priority and post-boys would gallop into stable yards shouting 'post haste' in order to attract attention and then swap their horse for a rested one to continue his journey. The same system was also the origin for the expression **By Return Post**, meaning immediate reply. A messenger who was asked to bring a reply to a letter back on his return journey was asked to wait until the recipient provided such a reply.

The **Pot Calling The Kettle Black** is one of the most frequently used idioms to describe a person pointing out his or her own flaws in somebody else. The allusion here is that in old households the cooking pots would be black iron and the kettles made of shining copper that would be cleaned regularly. The pot would be next to the kettle on a kitchen shelf and thus only able to see its own image reflected in the kettle's polished surface and would therefore assume the kettle too was dirty and black. In fact the pot would be accusing the kettle of a fault that only it had.

To **Ride Roughshod** over a person is to treat them harshly and without consideration of their feelings. Horses that are roughshod have nails deliberately left protruding from the shoe to provide extra grip in wet or icy conditions. To be trampled on or kicked by a horse with roughshod shoes would be uncomfortable to say the least. For a short time during the 1700s it became common practice for cavalry soldiers, from many countries, to ensure their horses were roughshod or had other sharp objects attached to their hooves. The idea was that during a charge the war-horses would cut and damage enemy mounts, but they soon found the shoes did as much damage to themselves and each other, so the practice was stopped.

The **Silly Season** is a period of time when most of the stories we hear are unlikely to be true, or something minor or superficial given undue prominence. The real silly season is during August and September when Parliament traditionally rises for its summer recess and MPs return to their constituencies. This deprives the newspapers of a steady stream of news: political rows, bad judgements, poor behaviour and general Westminster gossip. With big gaps in their publications to fill, journalists would make the most of silly stories, such as tales about the Loch Ness Monster, UFO sightings, giant marrows and student capers. One early story about a giant gooseberry led to the season being called the 'Big Gooseberry Season' but over time this became the 'silly season'.

To **Smell A Rat** is used when someone is suspicious of something, without actually having any demonstrable cause. In English towns and villages rats were a common problem and many people used dogs, whose highly sensitive sense of smell enabled them to sniff out rats and then kill the vermin. A person whose dog suddenly started sniffing around a house or barn would often say 'looks like he has smelled a rat', long before the pest could be seen or detected by humans.

The **Tip Of The Iceberg** is an expression used to emphasize the idea that what can be seen, or what has so far happened, is only a small part of the overall situation. Icebergs are typically found in the open seas, particularly around Greenland and Antarctica. They range in height, from the sea surface, from around only a few metres to as tall as 165m (550ft), the size of a 55-storey building. But the visible part is only around ten per cent of the overall size, so the tip of the iceberg is in no way the full picture.

If you find somebody **On The Warpath** it is better to stay well out of their way as it suggests they are in an aggressive mood and preparing for a fight. Before proper roads were mapped out the countryside was criss-crossed by bridle paths and other narrow ways. In North America feuding natives would regularly cross territories to confront their enemy, and the pathways flattened by foot soldiers and horsemen between the two camps quickly became known as 'war paths' as, essentially, the only time they were used was en route to war.

When a person **Wins His Spurs** he has achieved enough to earn the respect of his superiors and proved himself capable. In medieval England a boy born to noble families would have to first act as a pageboy before graduating to a squire when he was older. However, if a squire was to become one of the knights, he would have to distinguish himself on the battlefield in the service of his king. In this case the king, or other senior noblemen, would present the squire with a pair of golden spurs that would represent his elevation to the rank of knighthood. A spur is a small spiked wheel that horsemen would wear on their heels and use to 'spur' a horse along.

If I **Pull The Wool Over Your Eyes** I have tricked or deceived you. This expression is linked to the term **Bigwigs**. Centuries ago a man's status was confirmed by the size of his wig and such people were considered well worth robbing by the city scallywags and vagabonds. Some rogues developed the trick of approaching a victim from behind and pulling the wig down over a victim's eyes to disorientate him and make it easier to steal his possessions before running away.

17: MISCELLANEOUS

An **Acid Test** is the accepted process of finding out beyond any doubt if something is genuine or not. Gold is one of the few precious metals not affected by the majority of acids but it does react with a mixture of hydrochloric and nitric acids. When first used in the Middle Ages this mixture was given the Latin name 'Aqua Regia', meaning 'royal water', as it dissolved the king of metals. The first recorded use as an idiom was on 8 January 1918, as the First World War drew to a close, when US President Woodrow Wilson said to Congress, 'The treatment accorded Russia by her sister nations in the months to come will be an acid test of their goodwill.'

The 'acid test', or 'fizz test' as it has become known, is used these days mainly by geologists to differentiate between limestone and other types of rock.

A **Basket Case** is a light-hearted, although not entirely affectionate, way of describing somebody who cannot communicate properly, is mentally unstable and unable to cope emotionally. At the end of the First World War, the Surgeon General of the US Army was quoted in the *US Official Bulletin* (28 March 1919) that he 'denies there is any foundation for the stories being circulated of the existence of "basket cases" in our hospitals'. It is a clear reference to trench soldiers suffering shell shock and related mental illness. At the time basket weaving was a regular activity in both British and American mental hospitals, such as the one at Deolali (see **Doolally**). The phrase was known to be British Army slang during the First World War.

If a person is at your **Beck And Call** they are available to respond to your request at a moment's notice at any hour of the day or night. The word 'beck' is an old English word dating

back to the Middle Ages and it means to
summon, as a nobleman might summon a servant
with his finger. A beck could also be made with a
nod of the head or a wave of the hand, while
those out of sight would be summoned by a call.
So to be at a person's 'beck and call' basically
meant you were their servant. It is likely that the
word 'beckon' emerged from the phrase 'beck and
call' so while the word has evolved, the phrase
remains intact.

Some suggest that the real expression is 'beckon
call' and that over the years it has been misheard
or misspelled and corrupted, but evidence of the
word 'beck' from the 1300s suggests otherwise.
The Bible includes the line 'Christ's love is not at
the beck and call of our fluctuating affections,'
although nobody really knows to which edition it
was added or when.

Saved By The Bell – Although the phrase is
associated with boxing for obvious reasons, the
origin is supposed to lie at the Horse Guard
Parade in London. One night, during the
Victorian era, a guard was famously accused of
being asleep on duty. He denied the charge and
claimed he had heard the main bell of Big Ben

chime 13 times at midnight, instead of the usual 12. Such was the seriousness of the charge the clock mechanism was checked and it was discovered a cog was out of line and Big Ben would indeed chime 13 times instead of 12. On that evidence, the guard was freed – well and truly saved by the bell.

To suggest somebody has **Gone Round The Bend** is to unkindly infer they have gone mad. In the 1900s, the Victorians built hospitals in which to confine the mentally unsound. At the time stately homes were built with long, straight driveways in order that the building could be seen from the main road in all its splendour, albeit from a distance. The mental homes were placed at the end of long, curved driveways so that they would remain unseen, and therefore if a person had 'gone round the bend' it meant they had been confined.

To **Give Somebody A Break** means to give somebody an opportunity, usually after they have done something wrong or been perceived to do so. This phrase derives from the early street performers who would be given a break halfway through their act, during which they could pass a hat around and collect money for their performance. During the 19th century the phrase was picked up by the criminal and vagrant community who would pass a hat around each other for a friend on their release from prison so they would not have to return to the world totally penniless. That person was deemed to have been 'given a break'.

A **Busman's Holiday** means a person is spending his time away from work, doing exactly what he would during his working day. This idiom stems from the turn of the 20th century, when buses were horse-drawn. It was tradition that a bus driver would spend his days off travelling in the rear of his bus to make sure the relief driver was looking after his horses properly. As the horse was very much the means of his income, the animal's welfare was essential and drivers took few chances – even on their holidays.

A **Carbon Copy** is an exact duplicate of another thing. Until the development of personal computers and word processors, the tool of choice for writers and secretaries the world over was a typewriter. These used letter keys to punch words directly on to a sheet of paper and the only effective way of producing more than one copy at a time was to use a sheet of carbon paper placed between two or more sheets of writing paper. That way the pressure of the key would leave an imprint of whatever was written on the top page, on all the subsequent pages beneath the carbon.

Carbon paper was originally developed so that the blind would be able to write without the need for a pen or ink. Simply writing or drawing on the carbon sheet would leave a perfect image on the page beneath. A carbon copy was generally known as a c.c., which is why these letters are still used in emails. Blind carbon copies, where copies were sent without recipients knowing who else had received one, is the reason we use the letters b.c.c. in a similar way.

To be **In The Club** is to be pregnant. Between the two world wars Londoners began using the phrase 'she is in the Pudding Club', pudding being an old English slang word for semen.

Crocodile Tears are considered to be false tears or showing insincere sorrow. In fact, crocodiles, after eating, shed excess salt from glands located just beneath each eye, giving the impression of tears. According to ancient Egyptian legend, after the animal had devoured its victim it would immediately appear to be crying with remorse. The Egyptians coined the phrase and applied it to their double-dealing country folk who showed insincerity or false sorrow for their actions.

Digs is a word used to describe temporary accommodation or lodgings, usually for students. During the Californian gold rush, which began in 1849, miners raced to the area and had to live rough in shelters they dug for themselves into the hillsides. These became known as 'diggins'. Some enterprising folk dug out entire rows of them and rented out diggins to other prospectors arriving in the area. The term was shortened to 'digs' by the time it came into use in England a decade later.

To **Dish the Dirt** is to spread malicious gossip about another person. This is a gold-mining phrase (see also **Pan Out Nicely**) and alludes to a prospector swirling the dirt around in his pan before dishing it out and hopefully revealing the gold. The juicy gossip was the gold.

In the 17th century **The Dutch** were both military and trading rivals of England. The English attitude towards the Dutch can be found in the diaries of Samuel Pepys, whose work covered this period in English history. Such entries include 'several seamen came this morning and said they would go and do all they could against the Dutch' and 'And so to home where my heart aches as the Dutch have burned our ships.' It was common for the English to refer to the Dutch in derisory fashion and surprisingly many of the phrases continue to be used nearly 400 years later. Here are a few examples:

Ending an assurance with the suffix **'or I am a Dutchman'** implies total confidence in a suggestion or the one giving the guarantee will allow the recipient to call them a Dutchman, inviting the lowest form of insult. For example: 'My chickens are the finest in London sir, if I am found to be wrong then I'm a Dutchman.'

292

Dutch Auction – An auction that goes the wrong way, with the reserve figure being set too high in the first place and the auctioneer having to gradually decrease the price until a bid is finally made.

Dutch Bargain – A one-sided deal, and not a bargain at all.

Dutch Comfort – No real comfort at all.

Dutch Concert – An expression used to describe a shambles of a performance during which the singers sang different songs and the musicians played the wrong notes.

Dutch Courage – False bravery that has to be summoned up by alcohol.

Dutch Gold – A German alloy of copper and zinc which is gold in colour and often passed off as gold to unsuspecting dealers.

Dutch Party – Where the guests contribute their own food and drink.

Dutch Talent – Ability and results obtained through brawn rather than by intellect.

Dutch Treat – A gift for which the recipients pay themselves.

Dutch Uncle – A person who criticises severely, and often unfairly.

Double Dutch – A person speaking gibberish, which cannot be understood by an Englishman.

Triple Dutch – Like **Double Dutch**, only even more preposterous.

To **Go Dutch** means a gentleman expects his lady guest to pay for herself. Fair enough these days but not the behaviour of an English gentleman 400 years ago, the inference being that it was normal behaviour for a Dutchman.

Forking Out is used to describe handing over money, sometimes reluctantly. Many years ago the word fork was thieves' slang for finger and 'forking over' or 'forking out' became slang for paying or handing out money.

Funnybone – Nobody who takes a blow on the nerve between the elbow bones ever laughs; instead they experience a painful tingling sensation. So why is it called the 'funnybone'? The reason is a medical pun: the long bone in the upper arm connected by this nerve is called the 'humerus'. The joke stuck and had passed over into wider use by 1867.

Why do we say **Good Health** when we are about to drink alcohol, which is far from good for us? The answer lies in 19th-century England and the deadly outbreak of cholera between 1848 and 1849 in particular. In August 1849 cholera reached epidemic proportions in the Broadwick Street area of Soho in London, resulting in 344 deaths in only four days. But there were almost none in any neighbouring areas. Local physician Dr John Snow suggested cholera was linked to drinking polluted water and proved this when he found that 87 victims out of the 89 he examined were known to have drunk from the Broadwick Street well. Snow called for the authorities to take the handle off the pump, and almost immediately the outbreak was halted. For a long while afterwards the locals would avoid water and drink only ales and wines. When drinking they would toast each other with 'to your good health', knowing they were safe from the disease. Appropriately enough there is a pub called the John Snow on Broadwick Street today.

When we **Hedge Our Bets**, we are supporting more than one cause and increasing the possibility of a favourable outcome. The phrase is attributed to old English peasants and vagabonds who plied their trade overtly between or underneath hedges. Hedge was also a widely used expression applied to the lower classes. A 'hedge-priest' was a poor or untrustworthy man of the cloth, a 'hedge-writer' a Grub Street author and a 'hedge-marriage' was a clandestine union performed by a 'hedge-priest', possibly referring to a bigamous marriage. In 1811 the dictionary tells us the use of the word 'hedge' had become used as a term for protecting oneself against losses on a wager, suggesting that a gambler who 'hedges in' their bets is taking precautions against losses.

To find yourself **In A Hole** is to be in difficulty, particularly financially. American writer John P Quinn gave the best suggestion for this phrase in his 1892 book *Fools Of Fortune*. Poker tables in dimly lit gambling dens had a hole in the centre into which gamblers dropped a percentage of their stake money payable to the house. Losses to the dealer were also dropped into the hole, which was collected in locked iron boxes underneath. The owners would then collect their money at the end of each session. The expression is used these days to express any misfortune but back in the 19th century a losing gambler had all his money well and truly 'in the hole'.

In The Limelight implies being the centre of attention or in the public eye. When calcium oxide (lime) is heated, it produces a bright white light. In 1826 a Scottish army engineer called Thomas Drummond used this discovery to aid map-making in poor weather. The intense, highly visible limelight could be seen from a great distance and was used to mark out distances accurately. Shortly afterwards scientists developed his invention to produce other powerful lights, which were then used in lighthouses and later as spotlights in theatres, to focus attention on the main performer. So somebody who was standing 'in the limelight' was at the focus of attention.

Something **In A Nutshell** is explained in as few words as possible. Thousands of years ago important documents were carried around in walnut shells which would then be bound and kept waterproof. The idea of having something 'in a nutshell' means a shortened version that still covers every main point but there are examples of long and celebrated works being written in such small handwriting the document would still fit inside the shell of a walnut.

Something done **In A Jiffy** is done extremely quickly. 'Jiffy' might seem like a slang word but in fact it is a scientific term meaning 'unit of time'. Originally a jiffy was one sixtieth of a second, although it is now more commonly known as one hundredth of a second and occasionally even a millisecond. Some scientists use the word to describe the time light takes to travel one foot in a vacuum (a nanosecond). Whatever the duration, whenever we are told something will be done 'in a jiffy', it never is.

Jumping Over The Broomstick means a wedding that has taken place informally and without any real preparation. It started out as a custom for the medieval underclasses such as gypsies, wandering labourers and other people of no permanent address. All the happy couple had to do in bygone days was to jump together over a broomstick to secure their status as man and wife.

If someone got their **Just Deserts**, it is generally thought that they got what was coming to them, what they deserved. The confusion over the origins of this phrase lies in the spelling: 'deserts' is spelled like the word that means a vast sandy part of Egypt, but sounds like that spotted dick and custard we sometimes have after dinner, which is why the phrase is often explained as 'well, he deserved a pudding like that after what he did'.

When somebody is **Having Their Leg Pulled** they are on the receiving end of a deception, or a joke. An old Scottish rhyme dating from 1867 seems to reveal its origin with the lines 'He preached and at last pulled the auld body's leg, sae the Kirk got the gatherins o' our Aunty Meg.' The suggestion is that old Aunt Meg had been hanged for a crime and the preacher hauled on her legs to ensure she died quickly and without too much pain. Aunt Meg was known to have been the victim of much deception and trickery, which placed her at the gallows for a crime she did not commit, leading to the belief that having her leg pulled was the result of such deception.

To **Read Between The Lines** is to find the real message hidden away in a situation which is not at first obvious. The origin of this expression is found in cryptography and early attempts at passing coded messages. One method of secret writing was to place the real message on alternate lines and weave an unrelated story on to the other lines. On first reading a simple story or letter could be read, but only on reading the alternate lines could the hidden message be decoded.

People at **Loggerheads** are considered to be confronting each other. In the 15th and 16th centuries a 'logger' was the name given to a heavy wooden block fastened to the legs of grazing horses, enabling them to move slowly around a field but not to jump fences or stray too far. Frequently the loggers tangled with each other, leaving horses connected at close quarters and becoming agitated and hostile to each other. The phrase passed over into wider uses via Shakespeare's play *The Taming Of The Shrew*, during which two of the main characters are seen to be at 'loggerheads' with each other.

There is a second possible origin for the phrase dating to ancient nautical warfare. Sailors used a weapon called a loggerhead, which was a long pole with a cup fixed to the end. These were used to project flaming tar at enemy ships in close quarters to create injury and fire on board. Naturally both sides used similar weapons and such battles were known as 'being at loggerheads'.

Not to **Mince Your Words** is to speak plainly, frankly and with brutal honesty. The phrase is always used in the negative sense, as in 'not to' – we never hear complaints of somebody mincing their words. The first recorded use of the expression can be traced to 1649 and Joseph Hall's *Cases Of Conscience*. Some things we are told are unpleasant to swallow and difficult to digest, and the allusion is drawn from butchers who mince cheaper cuts of meat to make them easier to digest. A person 'not mincing his words' is not making any effort to soften their message.

Minding Your Ps And Qs is a gentle warning to behave in a correct and polite manner. There are two suggestions for the origin of this phrase and both have a reasonable claim. First up is the civilised surroundings of the French court during the 17th century. The aristocracy were expected to dance delicately when they took to the floor and dance instructors were in high demand. During their lessons pupils were encouraged to mind their 'pieds' (feet) and 'queues' (the tails of their wigs).

But my favourite can be found in the old London taverns, where the bartender would keep an account of how much beer their customers had been drinking by marking their pints under the letter P and their quarts (two pints) under the letter Q. Customers were well advised to watch their Ps and Qs to make sure they were not overcharged at the end of a session.

A **Movable Feast** is a regular event, although its date and time can be changed. This phrase is a religious expression used to describe important days in the calendar. Christmas and Boxing Day, for example, are immovable feasts. But Easter, an event determined by the lunar calendar, falls on a different date each year and is thus a movable feast. Any regular event, not necessarily religious, that can be changed, can be regarded as 'a movable feast'.

Mum's The Word means to convey no secrets and remain silent. This has nothing to do with mothers and more to do with the 'mmmm' we use with tightly closed lips indicating we have nothing to say on a subject. The phrase was first recorded in 1540 but is thought to be at least 200 years older still.

Mumbo Jumbo is the expression we use for language that seems nonsense and to have no discernible meaning. For the origin of this saying we travel to Africa with the explorers and missionaries of the 18th century. One of these travellers, Francis Moore, wrote a book of his adventures called *Inland Parts Of Africa*, published in 1738. In one part Moore includes the passage 'A dreadful bugbear to the women is called Mumbo Jumbo, which keeps the women in awe.'

Mumbo Jumbo was a legendary spirit in villages across Africa who was used by male tribal leaders in order to keep the women of their tribes in line. One of the major tribal customs was for a man to have several wives and bitching between them was a frequent occurrence. When an outbreak of backbiting became intolerable, the husband would dress up as Mumbo Jumbo and visit the main culprit in the dead of night and scare her rigid by shrieking and hollering. The trouble-making missus was then tied to a tree and given an old-fashioned thrashing by Mumbo Jumbo. Clearly he was not to be messed with. The phrase travelled back to England and became associated with the meaningless rantings of 'Mumbo Jumbo'.

Neither Fish Nor Flesh Nor Good Red Herrings means neither one thing nor the other. I realise this is not one of our better-known idioms but I hope you will forgive me for including it, for obvious reasons. Centuries ago it was a well-known and well-used expression, first recorded in 1528 when a person could be described as 'wone that is nether flesshe nor fisshe'. The rich would naturally eat meat (flesh) and the clergy would usually eat fish, but that left out the poor who would have to make do with dried and salted red herring.

John Dryden, in the epilogue to his play *The Duke of Guise* (1679) used the lines, 'Damn'd neuters in their middle way of steering, are neither fish nor flesh nor good red herring.' Which appears to confirm the expression is was in common use by the middle of the 17th century. Perhaps it could make a comeback?

A **Nest Egg** is a person's savings, which they will try to keep adding to. In the English countryside, prior to factory farming, chickens used to live naturally and lay their eggs in nests. To encourage hens to be more productive it was common practice for farmers to place a porcelain egg, known as a 'nest egg', into the breeding ground. Apparently it worked. Likewise, a small sum of money given to a person as a 'nest egg' was thought to encourage them to add to it.

To **Grasp The Nettle** is an expression used to describe facing an unpleasant task or problem with determination. Stinging nettles cause pain and discomfort when lightly touched or brushed against, but have been used over the centuries for their medicinal and nutritious content. The best way to collect nettles is to grab the leaf firmly; trying to do it softly or hesitantly will lead to a brush and an itchy rash or two.

To find somebody **As Drunk As A Newt** is never a pleasant experience, but at least they will be all right in the morning. But no one has ever found an intoxicated newt ricocheting up the high street on a Saturday night, so why the reference? It seems that during the 17th and 18th centuries 'newts' was the nickname gentlemen gave boys who looked after their horses while out on the town for the night. As they spent their evenings in gaming houses, bars and opium dens our forefathers were good enough to send out 'warm-up' drinks to the newts who would then usually be found rolling drunk by the time the horses were collected, hence the saying.

When somebody feels **As Right As Ninepence**, they are in tip-top condition and ready for anything. Silver ninepenny pieces were in common use in England until 1696, and were one of the highest-value coins in circulation. Also, the popular silver coin was often given as a token of love or affection and for those two reasons people were always pleased to have them. But some people believe the phrase is a simple corruption of the saying 'right as ninepins', which is a reference to the English pub game of skittles. Once the ninepins were all upright the game could begin.

To **Pay Through The Nose** is an odd expression. It is taken to mean we have paid a price far too high for goods or services. The origin of this lies in the Viking invasion of the British Isles during the ninth century. The Danes had particularly strict tax laws, which were applied with relish every time they invaded a foreign land. In Ireland the Vikings levied an especially high tax which they called the 'Nose Tax'. The reason for that was any citizen failing to pay had their nose either slit open or cut off altogether. This charming behaviour continued until the genial Viking leader, Eric Bloodaxe, was killed by the English warrior King Edred at the Battle of Stainmore in 954.

The expression **To The Nth Degree** literally means 'to any extent' possible. We will go as far as we possibly can to achieve a result. This is a well-known mathematical expression where the letter 'n' denotes an indefinite number. In numerical circles there is no limit to the nth degree.

When something is said to happen **Once In A Blue Moon** it isn't going to happen very often. The inference is that it never will. This has nothing to do with the actual colour of the moon or that on rare occasions light reflecting through smoke and dust particles can cause a warm blue glow around the surface, as after the eruption of Krakatoa in 1883 when the moon looked blue for nearly two years.

Instead, the origin of the phrase can be found in the lunar cycles. There is a full moon in each month and all 12 have names: the Harvest Moon, the Hunter's Moon, the Hay Moon and so on. The dates on which these full moons are due to appear are listed in red in the *Maine Farmers Almanac*. However, approximately seven times in every 19 years there will be 13 full moons in a given year. This means that for one month in around 33 there are two full moons, the second of which doesn't have a formal name. This moon is listed in blue, not red, in the Almanac and so it became known as the blue moon – the one you have to wait a long time for.

The expression **Pardon My French** is often used to excuse foul or offensive language. The Hundred Years War was a series of conflicts between the French and the English that lasted from 1337 until 1453 (116 years). The rivalry between the two countries was bitter and intense and lasted for many centuries even after the fighting had died down. During this period the English public regarded their enemy as a vulgar and rude race, so swear words were widely dismissed as being French in origin.

When something has gone **Pear Shaped** it has gone wrong, or at least not quite according to plan. The 1940 film *My Little Chickadee,* starring WC Fields and Mae West, contains the line 'I have some very definite pear-shaped ideas' and the phrase certainly originates around that time. However, it is widely thought that early RAF pilots are responsible for popularising it. While practising loops a trainee pilot would often fail to make a perfect circle and would flatten the plane's flight during the bottom section. These mistakes were referred to as 'going pear shaped'.

When the **Penny Finally Drops** it means somebody has finally understood something. This saying dates back to the Victorian era and the popular penny slot arcades. Often, in the old wooden slot machines, the penny would stick halfway down and users would have to either wait or give the machine a thump before the 'penny finally dropped' and they could start the game.

Pin Money is now used as a term for small amounts of money, but the sum was not always small. In the 14th and 15th centuries pins were very expensive and only allowed to be sold on the first two days of January. Husbands gave their wives money saved for the purchase. As time went by pins became ever cheaper and the money could be spent on other things. However, the expression remained.

Pull The Other One might be said as an expression of scepticism, or to indicate not being taken in by a joke. Starting life as the longer 'Pull the other one, it's got bells on', the phrase probably refers to jesters', fools' or jokers' costumes, which often had bells attached and were used to delight the crowds in Victorian theatres. The expression is probably just an extension of the earlier **Having Your Leg Pulled**, when you are thought to be on the receiving end of a deception or a joke.

To **Rob Peter To Pay Paul** is to take or borrow from one source to contribute to another, thereby solving one problem but creating another. Use of this expression is traceable back to 17 December 1540 when the church of St Peter in Westminster, London, became a cathedral. But its elevated status lasted only 10 years when the diocese of Westminster was placed back under the authority of St Paul's Cathedral and St Peter's became merely a church again. To **add insult to injury**, much of the land and property of St Peter's was then sold off to fund repairs to St Paul's. There was public outcry at the robbing of St Peter's to prop up St Paul's, and the expression became popularised.

311

There is, however, evidence that the phrase dates back centuries earlier. This is provided by the Oxford priest and theologian John Wyclif, who wrote in 1380, 'How should God approve that you rob Peter and give this robbery to Paul in the name of Christ?' (*Select Works III*). While it is possible that 16th-century Londoners applied this phrase to the events surrounding their cathedrals, it is clear that the phrase had been coined in the mid- to late-1400s.

Ruling The Roost is a phrase used to suggest a person is in charge and demonstrating their authority. The obvious allusion is to a chicken run, where the cockerel rules over all the hens. But not so fast. The phrase has been in use since the 16th century and was popularised by Shakespeare when he wrote in *Henry VI Part II* (1590): 'Suffolk, that new made man that rules the roast.' Indeed, tradition has it that the master of the house carves and serves the roast meat and in 1637 Thomas Nabbes wrote in *Microcosmus*, 'I am my lady's cook, and king of the kitchen where I rule the roast.' This origin is further supported by the fact that in Anglo-Saxon English the word roast was pronounced with a long 'o', so it sounded like roost.

So it seems that in days gone by, ruling the roast was indeed a demonstration of authority.

The phrase **Above** or **Below The Salt** describes a person's status. This phrase comes straight from the great banqueting rooms where the silver salt cellars would be placed in the centre of the table. Those sitting on the same side of the salt as the host (above it) were considered the most important guests and those further away (below) were less valued guests.

To be **In Seventh Heaven** is to be truly delighted, over the moon and on cloud nine. According to Muslim beliefs there are seven heavens, each of them relating to one of the seven planets ruling the universe. The suggestion is that every level of heaven consists of a precious stone or metal and a servant of the Most High inhabits each one. The seventh heaven is considered the most glorious and is occupied by Abraham who presides over everything and who is the most loyal to God. During the Middle Ages the Cabbalists, who were Jewish mystics steeped in the occult, reinforced this belief by interpreting the seventh heaven as the domain of God and his holy angels. Therefore to be 'in seventh heaven' is to be in a place of eternal bliss.

A **Shaggy Dog Story** is a story of unconvincing origin, not necessarily to be believed. The origin of this phrase is, in fact, a real shaggy dog story which, when told on the London social scene during the 1800s, wasn't believed by everybody but is still a good story. Apparently a wealthy gentleman, who owned a grand residence in Park Lane, lost his beloved shaggy dog during a walk across Hyde Park opposite his home. The man was heartbroken and advertised extensively in *The Times* for the return of his companion. An American living in New York heard the news and took pity on the dog's owner. He vowed he would search for a pet matching the description of the lost hound and deliver it to London on his next business visit, which he duly did. But when the New Yorker presented himself at the London mansion he was met by a po-faced butler who looked down at the dog, winced and exclaimed, 'But not as shaggy as that, sir!' The story caused howls of laughter across London's social circuit, but was not entirely believed by everybody. A 'shaggy dog story' indeed.

To **Get Shirty** means to become aggressive and look for an argument or a fight. This phrase has a direct link back to the 18th century when it was customary for a gentleman to remove his shirt before engaging in fisticuffs, ensuring it remained clean, tear-free and could be worn again afterwards.

To give a person **Short Shrift** is to dismiss their opinions or feelings without much consideration. The word 'shrift' means a confession given to a priest, after which absolution is given. It derives from the verb 'shrive' meaning 'to hear a confession', and its past tense is 'shrove' as in Shrove Tuesday, the day prior to Lent when pious folk attend confession. During the 17th century, when criminals were taken out and executed almost immediately after the ultimate sentence was passed, they were given a few moments to save their souls by confessing their sins to a waiting priest. This was usually on the gallows platform and time would have been short, which is how the phrase 'short shrift' passed over into wider use.

To **Sleep Tight** is to sleep well and have a good night's rest. In this context the word 'tight' is generally thought to be about pulling the bedclothes tightly around ourselves. But the first beds to be mass-produced in England were made with straw mattresses held by criss-crossed ropes attached to the bed frames. Sooner or later the ropes would slacken off and the mattress would become uncomfortable. For this reason all beds were sold with an iron tool, similar to a large clothes peg, which was used to wind the ropes tighter whenever they became loose. Therefore to suggest a person 'sleeps tight' was to remind them to tighten their mattress ropes and have a more comfortable bed to sleep in.

To **Get Hold Of The Wrong End Of The Stick** means to misunderstand something entirely and to misinterpret a situation. The phrase can be traced back to the 1400s and began life as 'the worse end of the staff' (or lance), with the wording changing during the 1800s. It is also said to date back to Roman times and their use of communal toilets where people sat side by side. For personal hygiene reasons the Romans used a short staff with a sponge tied to one end and everybody took great care not to get hold of the wrong end when reaching out to use it. Not only did they give us roads, sanitation and great architecture, but also, it appears, an early version of Andrex.

To **Up Sticks** is to leave a place and move on to pastures new. There are several suggestions for the origin of this phrase. One is that in the days of horse travel a mount would be tethered to the ground by a picket (rope) tied to a stick driven into the earth. These sticks would be carried around by horsemen and used whenever they arrived at a place, upping them again on departure. Alternatively, a ship's mast was known as a stick, and when they were raised the vessel was ready to depart. Either way the phrase is relatively recent and first recorded during the 1800s.

Why do we call a level of a building a '**Storey**'? The word 'story' derives from the ancient Greek word 'historia' meaning 'account of events'. Back in the 14th century, the word 'story' was used in architecture in the sense that stained glass windows and stone carvings or sculptures on the outside of a building had real stories as their theme. The more rows of pictures, the more stories they told. The higher the window or the building, the more stories it could have. This developed in time to mean an entire level of a building was known as a storey.

Straight From The Horse's Mouth is a term used to describe accurate, first-hand information. In bygone days a horse was a valuable commodity and there were few ways of reliably assessing a horse's age before buying one. Everybody was afraid of spending good money on an old horse with very little work left in it. One of the better ways of reassurance was to look at the teeth of the animal and find out how far they had worn, or how far its gums had receded, to determine the age of a nag. First-hand inspection would reveal the truth. **Don't Look A Gift Horse In The Mouth** is directly related to the same practice. It was regarded as extremely rude to check the teeth of a horse (to see if it was worth anything) if it had been given as a gift.

There But For The Grace Of God Go I is used by people noting another's misfortune and suggesting it could easily have befallen themselves. The popular Protestant preacher John Bradford first used this phrase while being held in the Tower of London on the trumped-up charges of 'trying to stir up a mob'. In fact, all he had done was to save a Catholic preacher named Bourne from a baying Protestant mob. But this happened during the reign of Mary I, whose restoration of the Catholic Church saw the persecution of many Protestants. While in the Tower, Bradford witnessed many being taken away for execution and each time would remark, 'There but for the grace of God goes John Bradford.' But Bradford was soon charged with heresy and later burned at the stake in Smithfield market on 1 July 1555.

To **Tie The Knot** is commonly understood to mean marriage. The phrase means very little to any western wedding ceremony, but we can find it in many other cultures around the world. In Sikh weddings both the bride and groom wear silk scarves and the bride's father knots them together as the happy couple honour the Sikh scriptures. Chinese Buddhists honour the deity Yue Laou by uniting couples with a silken cord after which nothing can break their unity, and during Hindu ceremonies several garments of the committed are tied together as they walk around a holy fire. In western ceremonies the knot has a much lower-key role as it is only the ribbons of a bridal bouquet that are tied together. In all cases the knot is there to symbolise love, unity and a bond that cannot ever be broken in any circumstances. (The divorce lawyers can stop laughing right now.)

Once a thing is **Up The Spout** it is gone and lost forever. A spout was a tube found in pawnbroker shops or bookmaker's. Articles to be pawned, or wagers placed, would be put into the spout and whisked off to the office above where it was safely stored away. It was commonly known for a man's weekly wages to have gone 'up the spout' before the weekend was over, or for an object of value to go the same way during troubled times.

Upper Crust is an expression used to describe England's upper or ruling classes. The origin of this phrase dates back as far as the mid-14th century when the upper, crusty part of a loaf of bread would be reserved for the master of the house and his honoured guests, while the softer underside was given to the minions. It became widely used in America in the early 18th century when it was applied to the 'upper layers' of society.

When something has **Gone To The Wall** it is finished, over and can never be recovered. This phrase apparently has a rather morbid origin and relates to the practice of placing the dead next to the churchyard wall bordering the graveyard, prior to a funeral service. But there are other suggestions for its use in our language. Four hundred years ago the city streets were narrow and unlit, and invited crime. After dark, innocent passers-by were always at risk from thieves or muggers and a person cornered in a dark alley with their back to the wall really was vulnerable.

Another suggested origin comes from medieval chapels, such as the one found in Dover Castle, which provided stone seating around the walls to support the elderly and infirm. The rest of the congregation were required to stand and the expression used at the time was that 'the weak had gone to the wall'. Take your pick from those.

To ask for something **Warts And All** is to require that no attempt be made to cover any defects or hide unsavoury detail. Oliver Cromwell was a radical parliamentarian who overthrew the English monarchy in the mid-17th century. At the time portrait painters would soften the features of their subjects by removing blemishes and facial lines from their work (a sort of early air-brushing) and the end result would always be flattering. But when Cromwell, as Lord Protector, commissioned Sir Peter Levy to paint his portrait, he issued the artist with the following instructions: 'I desire you would use all your skill to paint my picture truly like I am and not flatter me at all. Remark all these roughness, pimples, warts and everything as you see me, otherwise I will never pay you a farthing for it.' The end result does include a large wart, just below Cromwell's lower lip.

A **Wheeler Dealer** is a crafty business person with an eye for a quick profit, possibly dishonest. It is possible the phrase originates in the gambling casinos or saloons where roulette is played on a wheel and dealers handle cards. In this context a 'wheeler dealer' could be a professional gambler, therefore having no established profession or trade.

However, there is a second possibility. Billings-gate Fish Market in London was once one of the busiest markets in England and a place where underhand business often took place. In the days before automated transport, the barrows loaded with fresh fish would be wheeled up from the dockside so that the dealing could take place. It is thought the fishmongers at Billingsgate were known as 'wheeler dealers'.

To **Whet Your Appetite** is to have your interest and enthusiasm aroused, and not only for food. In bygone days knives and tools were sharpened on a type of grindstone called a whetstone, so anything that has been 'whetted' has been sharpened.

To have a **Whip Round** is to take an informal collection, usually for money to buy a collective gift or make a donation. This phrase comes from a combination of sources, namely the British Parliament, an army officers' mess and the hunting ground. The phrase 'whipper-in' is still used in fox-hunting circles as the name for a huntsman's assistant who keeps the hounds in their pack by using a whip. In the mid-1800s this phrase was shortened to 'the whip' and later broadened again to 'whip-up' meaning to generate enthusiasm or interest. In Parliament those appointed by a party to keep members in line and ensure they vote for the right motions are still known as 'The Whips'. Army officers, no doubt with a hunting background, extended this phrase even further during their long nights socialising in the officers' mess. At official dinners for large gatherings, officers solved the problem of who would pay for the large rounds of wine by assigning an orderly in the role of a whip. He would go around the table collecting sums from each gentleman in a wine glass and then be sent off to pay for further rounds. This became known as a 'whip round' and that is how it passed over into the English language. It was further established in 1861 when Thomas Hughes wrote in his novel *Tom Brown At Oxford*, 'If they would stand a whip of ten shillings a man then they may have a new boat.'

A **Whipping Boy** is a person who takes the punishment for a misdemeanour committed by somebody else. In the Middle Ages it was quite common for a boy of ordinary, or even peasant, stock to be educated alongside a prince or the sons of the aristocracy. As a result the commoner benefited from great privileges and in some cases the position was sought after. However, there was a down side. It was considered inappropriate for a schoolmaster or tutor to punish a member of the aristocracy and in the case of a prince he simply would not dare. Instead, when the toff misbehaved or failed in his studies, it would be the innocent commoner who received a thrashing in his place. But there are well-recorded exceptions. When George Buchanan, the Latin master to King James I, decided the boy needed punishing, he thrashed the prince himself, despite the presence of a whipping boy. The brave Buchanan threatened to do it again if the misdemeanour was repeated.

The practice wasn't confined to the schoolroom. When the French King Henry IV converted to Catholicism in 1593 he sent two ambassadors to the Pope who were symbolically whipped to atone for the King's previous Protestantism. They were both well rewarded and made cardinals soon afterwards.

As Clean As A Whistle is known to mean bright, shiny and spotless. It could also mean untarnished in the sense of getting away from something 'as clean as a whistle'. There are several suggestions for the root to this phrase. One is the bright shiny locomotive with its polished brass whistle. Others point to a freshly carved wooden whistle or to the sound a shining sword makes as it swishes through the air.

A **White Elephant** is an expression used to describe something useless that has, or will, become a huge burden to those who possess it. For this we travel to Thailand, in the days when it was known as Siam. According to the legend white elephants were so highly prized that whenever one was discovered it automatically belonged to the King. It was considered a serious offence to neglect, put to work or even to ride a white elephant so they were of no use to an owner, yet still highly revered. The King, it appears, was a wily old devil and used them in ruthless fashion. He decided that any subject causing him displeasure would be given a white elephant as a special royal gift. The subject was obviously unable to refuse a royal gift but the beast had to be cared for and could not be made to pay its way. Such gifts could ruin a man financially. The phrase arrived in England in the mid-18th century after the Empire builders brought it home with them, applying it to expensive but otherwise useless public buildings or monuments.

To be awarded the **Wooden Spoon** doesn't say much about your performance as it is given to those who finish last. The custom began in 1811 at Cambridge University where each year there were three classes of honours degrees awarded. The first class winners were called Wranglers, and said to have been born with golden spoons in their mouths. Following them were the Senior Optimes (silver spoons) and the third class went to the Junior Optimes (lead spoons). The last of the Junior Optimes was called the 'wooden spoon' and the University adopted the custom of presenting a wooden spoon to the graduate who had the lowest exam result in the Maths Tripos. But it was still a pass!

INDEX TO PHRASES